Happy Days on Paige Hill

by Mildred Rumney Morgrage

Order this book online at www.trafford.com
or email orders@trafford.com

Most Trafford titles are also available at major online book retailers.

Note for Librarians: A cataloguing record for this book is available from Library
and Archives Canada at www.collectionscanada.ca/amicus/index-e.html   .

Printed in Victoria, BC, Canada.

ISBN: 978-1-4269-1721-9

*Our mission is to efficiently provide the world's finest, most comprehensive book publishing
service, enabling every author to experience success. To find out how to publish your book, your
way, and have it available worldwide, visit us online at www.trafford.com*

Trafford rev. 10/1/09

 www.trafford.com

North America & international
toll-free: 1 888 232 4444 (USA & Canada)
phone: 250 383 6864 ♦ fax: 812 355 4082

*This book was written in loving
remembrance of "Josie", and
is dedicated To Flora and Florence,
all who are left of "The Paige Girls,"
to whose constant urging and
encouragement I owe any success
it may have.*

Mildred Rumney Morgrage

Paige Family

John G. Paige – Nancy Campbell
b. June 10, 1803   d. abt 1866
d. Jul 17, 1859   d. May 29, 1880
son

Samuel C. Harrington – Nancy Hasting
b. abt 1817   b. abt 1829

daughter

David A. Paige
b. Mar 30, 1842
d. Jun 3, 1914

Ella F. Harrington
b. Aug. 13, 1853

CHILDREN OF DAVID AND ELLA

Josephine E. Paige   b. June 12, 1874 d. 1 Feb. 1940
David E. Paige   b. October 4, 1876
Jennie M. Paige   b. June 30, 1879 d. 25 Nov 1945
Flora A. Paige   b. March 16, 1883 d. 15 Feb 1951
Edith Paige   b. May 10, 1885 d. July 11, 1885
Florence Paige   b. October 28, 1886 d. Nov. 1982
Bertha R. Paige   b. September 10, 1888 d. 14 Oct 1937

Chapter 9

GOFFSTOWN, NEW HAMPSHIRE 1880

A little girl stood with her nose pressed against the window of a train whizzing along on its way northward from Boston. She gazed inquiringly at every house and town they passed, often turning to her mother to ask – "Is that Goffstown, mama?" And her mother would patiently reply, "No, Millie, I've told you we have to reach Manchester first, and then go on another train. It is quite a way yet."

It seemed an endless trip to the restless little girl, altho', as a matter of fact, it was only about sixty miles. But at long last, of course, they reached Manchester and rose to leave the train, and a hard time her mother had to keep Millie's hand firmly in hers until the train actually stopped.

The conductor had been much amused at the child's evident excitement on the trip and as he helped them down the high steps, he said, "Well, here you are at last, young lady, safe and sound in Manchester. You'll find the train to Goffstown right over there." And he pointed to a short train puffing away on a side track. "You've got plenty of time; it doesn't start for ten minutes yet."

"How far is it to Goffstown, Mr. Conductor?" piped Millie, and he laughed and said, "Only about eight miles. Won't take long to get there." And then he bellowed, "ALL ABOARD!! ALL ABOARD!!" He stepped aboard his train, waved his hand to the engineer, and off the train went.

Millie hurried her mother across to the Goffstown train, which was really the New Boston train, and very soon it, too, started off, puffing and snorting, toward their destination.

Millie was perfectly sure that Goffstown was going to be a wonderful place, a farm, flowers, grass, trees, cows, hens, and best of all, three children to play with! No wonder she was anxious to get there!

While the train is poking along, for this was no fast express like the one from Boston, let us find out a little about Millie, and how it happened that she was on her way to the country.

She was "half past six," as she expressed it when asked her age, and had been born and always lived in Boston. She was very small for her age, and had never been a strong child, and being their only one, this was a constant worry to her father and mother. She was thin and pale, not at all a pretty child, but for all her delicacy, she was spirited, full of fun, high strung and very active.

Every spring their doctor advised the country for the summer, and this year he had been especially insistent about it. "If you want to keep her, get her out of the city!" he had said "Take her to a real farm, where there are children if possible. Let her run loose, and I mean loose!" he went on. "Go barefooted, lots of play, no more discipline than necessary, lots of milk and eggs, - but mostly freedom." He felt that Mrs. Rumney was a thoroughly good woman, but that she expected too much of the child and believed in too strict a regime.

But Mrs. Rumney was wholly at a loss as to where such a place as he recommended could be found. She had spent the last two summers at country places found through advertisements, but had been disappointed so far as any improvement in the child's health went.

She disliked country life herself, never felt safe away from a city, and she certainly had never allowed Millie to "run loose" as Dr. Street had expressed it.

Millie's father, however, had been born and raised on a farm, prior to his serving through the Civil War and he knew about what the doctor meant. However, he knew of no such place and was as much at a loss as his wife. But Millie was the idol of his heart, and, terrified at the thought of possibly losing her, he declared that such a place must be found, and that the advice as to "running loose" was to be followed to the letter.

A piece of good fortune came their way, for one afternoon a friend came to call, and upon hearing of their quandary, exclaimed that she believed she knew of exactly such a place!

"It is a beautiful place, a farm, in Goffstown, New Hampshire. Mrs. Paige was a schoolmate of mine in Manchester, and married and moved there. It is way up on a hill, and they have cows and hens. She has three lovely children, the oldest a few month's younger than Millie. She never has taken boarders but perhaps she would. I can write her, if you'd like to have me."

So the matter was arranged and presently Mrs. Paige had written saying they could come for the summer "if they would take things as they were." Stating that they lived very simply, with plain, wholesome food, and all the milk, cream and eggs they could want.

Mrs. Rumney accepted gladly, and it was finally settled that they should come early in June, as soon as school was done.

And so here they were, well on their way, Millie still gazing out the car window, at a jolly rippling little river running parallel with the tracks, deep in a rocky gully.

She did not know, then, that just before reaching Goffstown, she could have looked across the Intervale and the river and on to hills in the distance, and actually have seen the little house and big barn to which she was bound! Not far as the crows fly, but a long way the way they were obliged to go.

Suddenly the train whistled briskly, the conductor called "Goffstown – Goffstown – next station, Goffstown!" They racketed through a covered bridge, over the river, and finally stopped at the little brown depot.

A few moments later they stood on the narrow platform, a crowd of several villagers, who always assembled, just as they do in most small towns, "to see the train come in."

A tall, tow-headed young man, a typical farmer, with a pleasant smile and kind blue eyes, stepped forward, wide straw hat in hand. He asked if they were bound for Paige hill, and upon being told they were, ushered them round to the back of the Depot and helped them up to the high seat of a Democrat wagon.

"I'd-a come in the buggy," he explained, "only I thought likely you'd have a trunk, and we could take it right along with us." And as Mrs. Rumney handed him her trunk check, he disappeared into the freight room much to her consternation, for she noticed that the horse was not tied, and the seat seemed terribly high up in the air – much too high to jump from in case the horse should start.

But Samson had no idea of starting up till he had to, - in fact, he was glad to stand quietly in the shade, for he had been working all forenoon. He didn't even move when the trunk was slammed into the back of the wagon, and took his time about it when his master climbed in and slapped his back with the reins, saying "Come on you, Samson! Git along if you want your dinner!"

"I'm Joe Gilmore," he said affably, as they turned into the pretty, tree shaded main street. "Live on the next farm beyond the Paiges. Ella couldn't very well come down to meet you herself, so she asked me to do it. You've come to a mighty nice place an' mighty nice people. Nice little town, too, least ways we think so. That there's the Congregational Church – and that's Parker's store. Quite a store too. You can git most anything you want to at Parker's. It's the post office too." And then suddenly he added, "How'd you like to drive awhile, little girl?"

"Oh!" exclaimed Mrs. Rumney, horrified at the very idea. "Why! She never drove a horse in her life!" But Joe only laughed comfortable. "Time she did, then," and he settled Millie back on the seat between them and put the reins into her willing hands. "She can drive ole Samson all right – all she's got to do is hold the reins. Children all love to drive."

"But she might drop them!" Mrs. Rumney replied, none too easy on the high seat and dismayed at the idea of Millie at the reins.

"Wunt do no harm if she does," Joe calmly responded. "He'd just go right along, or stop. Half the time I just leave 'em wound round the whip socket, and he jest 'mangs' right along." Then seeing she still looked worried, he added, "Ain't no corner to be turned for a mile yet, not 'till we reach John Whipples, an' I'll take the reins then."

So presently, seeing that old Samson "just 'manged' right along" paying no attention whatever to Millie's light slaps of the reins on his fat back, she relaxed and paid more attention to the pleasant countryside through which they were passing. Occasionally they caught a glimpse of the shining tumbling little river, the Piscataquog, and two beautiful green mountains beyond, which Joe told them were the Uncanoonucs. He told them too, that sometimes the neighbors drove up the further one and had picnics on the summit. (Today (early 1900's) there is a good road, a cog railroad and ski trail on the mountain, but in those days there was nothing but a rough wood road.)

When they reached Whipple's corner and started up the hill for the half mile yet to go, true to his word Joe took the reins, consoling Millie by telling her she'd be going to the village with him often, as Bert and Josie did, and that they could take turns driving. "And besides," he added, "you can run up to our place with Bert most any afternoon and ride ole Samson down to the watering trough." So Millie yielded the reins with no fuss, much to her mother's relief.

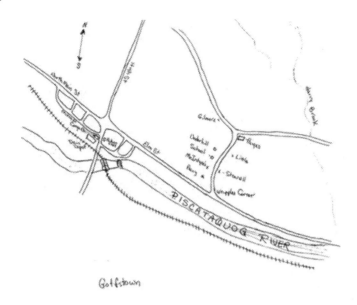

Goffstown

There were more houses on this road, which rose steadily higher and higher, and Joe gave them a brief and general history of each house as they passed. The first was quite the tiniest house they had ever seen, perched way up on a rise on the left and quite a distance from the road. "Pecoy Place." Joe informed them. "Miz Pecoy's a nice ole body, got three girls, two of 'em long in their teens, and one' bout six or seven, just right to play with you Millie," he added, having caught her name by this time.

Then another house, not much larger, but sitting nearer the road, and with a huge old barn in the field behind it. "McIntyre's" Joe said, waving to a bearded old man who stood beside a wall near the house. "Nice folks got a daughter, young lady named Lois. She's full of fun and you'll like her – her mother too, mighty fine old lady."

Then on the right, a large, well kept house and farm buildings, "Stowell's" Joe said. But Millie wasn't interested as he had added "no children there."

And presently they passed a small red building on the left up on quite a rise, and with a rough stony yard in front. Attached to it was a small, unpainted shed. "School house," said Joe tersely. "That's where Josie and Bert go, come fall." Millie stared wonderingly at it, wholly unable to picture it as a school house – just a tiny, one story building, with only a door and window facing the road. She wondered how many children it could hold and decided not even half as many as in her class at the big school in Boston.

One smaller house just beyond it sat side-wise to the road, and Mrs. Rumney began wondering if the Paige house was as small as most houses they had passed, and if so, how could she make room for two extra people!

"That's Helen Underhill's" Joe said. "Got a boy about Bert's age, and they are great chums" Just as he spoke a tow-headed boy rushed round the corner, stared a moment, and then yelled, "hey Joe!"

"Hey yourself and see how you like it," returned Joe, "Better go up to Bert's this afternoon and meet the new folks." To Millie's indignation the boy replied, rubbing one bare foot over the other, "Don' wanter meet no girls – got enuff round here now," and dashed round the corner again.

"Huh! He'll be up just the same," said Joe, laughing at Millie's scowling face. "Over there is Walker Little's" he went on, pointing to a large white house and red barn on the right. And then to Mrs. Rumney's relief, for she was tired of the long ride and hard seat, he added, "and the next place is Paige's."

Millie's scowl vanished, and she straightened up, looking expectantly ahead. She saw a small white house, larger than some they had passed however, set well back on a wide green lawn, dotted with beautiful maple trees. Across the road stood a large, unpainted barn in which, although she hardly noticed it at all at the moment, she was to have many wonderful times in the years that followed.

Her main attention was given to a plump, sweet-faced woman and little girl, who stood on the big door rock at the door of the house. There was only six month's difference in the ages of the two children, but considerable difference in their looks, for Josie was large for her age, and fat and rosy with health – wonderful pink cheeks, bright hazel eyes, and a mass of beautiful reddish brown wavy hair.

The two little girls stared at each other with inquiring eyes, presently smiling at one another – and then and there began a friendship that lasted, in spite of childish quarrels occasionally, for more than sixty years.

Mrs. Paige, who almost immediately became "Aunt Ella" to the little city girl, stepped forward to lift her down, but stopped abruptly, aghast at such a tiny, frail looking child. Long afterwards, she confessed that she had actually felt afraid to handle her! "Why she looked as if she would break if you touched her!" she said. She admitted, too, that when Joe had helped Mrs. Rumney down, she wondered if she had two invalids to board! No wonder, perhaps, for both were thin and pale, and of course, tired from the long trip.

Aunt Ella, while a small woman herself, was round and plump and brown as a berry. She thought they both looked half starved, and altho' she knew that such was not the case, she mentally determined to "feed tham ip and get some flesh on their bones!"

Bert, who had been hiding behind the barn door, was peeking out at the new comers. Like Frank, he wished Millie might have been a boy instead of "jest another girl!" A boy would have been more fun to play and do "stunts" with. But they needn't have worried, for they soon found that she was quite a "Tom Boy", which is next best to being a real one, you know. And, too, they learned that there were few stunts they could do, that Millie couldn't master, and that quite often she produced one they flunked completely!

A little later, as they sat down to a bountiful dinner Bert sidled in, for like most boys, he was always hungry. For a little while he was shy and speechless, giving strict attention to his well filled plate, but as Josie and Millie were chattering away like magpies, he soon joined in.

Aunt Ella was distressed at her guests' poor appetites, but she assured them that being out of doors a lot and the good fresh air would soon remedy that. She was right, too, for "Aunt Nellie," as she was soon called, almost lived out of doors, and was soon taking walks, or picking berries with Aunt Ella, and began actually looking forward to meal hours.

And Millie! She ran and romped and played all day long, and in almost no time at all was "racing" Bert, to see who could eat the most of this or that. She even ate potatoes, which she had never liked. The children had been amazed one day, when she remarked calmly, "I bet my pappa'll be 'sprised to see me eating potatoes! He used to give me a nickel if I'd eat a whole one – but I wouldn't very often.

"Wouldn't eat a potato – for a NICKEL?" Josie exclaimed, and Bert piped up, "Golly! I'd eat a whole PECK of potatoes for a nickel!"

And to her mother's delight, she ate her cereal every morning without the least fuss, which had always been a "must" before. And although she really never learned to love milk, she drank a full glass at dinner and supper, simply because the other children did. There was always a big white pitcher full on the table.

It had horrified Aunt Ella to learn that she expected and was given coffee at breakfast. Josie and Bert were allowed to have it on Sunday mornings, as a special treat, but even then she saw that it was mostly cream. And gradually she did like- wise with Millie, who never seemed to notice that she was really drinking cream diluted with coffee!

And day by day the two showed results. Their cheeks rounded out, they lost their city pallor, and grew brown and rosy. Aunt Nellie lost the worried, harried look in her big eyes and Millie grew freckled as well as brown, and was happy the whole day long.

And now let us leave them at their first dinner in Goffstown, and get acquainted with Jennie, and with "Uncle David," although he was not present that day.

Jennie was the baby, a little over two years old, and a beautiful baby she was too, fat and roly-poly, with shining bright brown eyes, pink cheeks and a mass of light brown hair. Her little white teeth gleamed when she smiled, which was practically all the time, for a better natured baby never lived.

Uncle David worked in Manchester during the week, coming home Saturday afternoons. He went back Sunday evenings, and to Aunt Nellie's surprise, - walked! Eight miles seemed an impossible walk to her, but he declared he got used to it marching during the War, and that he thoroughly enjoyed it! He was a very large man, six feet tall and with wide shoulders. His eyes were deep set and dark, and always seemed to be twinkling under his heavy brows, and he wore a dark mustache. Bert was very like him and grew more so with every passing year.

At first Millie stood a little in awe of him, not knowing quite how to take his dry way of teasing, so different from her father's gay and merry ways. But she soon grew used to him, and would go tearing down the road with Josie and Bert, when he came in sight Saturday afternoons. They always watched for him, and raced off to cling to his arms and legs, trying to locate the box of candy he never failed to bring.

Now that we know these two, the family is complete, and we can go back to the dinner table and see what has happened.

eggs = ice cream or fishhooks or candy or crayons

Chapter II

Dinner was over, Aunt Nellie had gone upstairs to rest a little and unpack the trunk. Jennie had been put to bed for her nap, and Aunt Ella was busying herself with household duties, so the three children were left to themselves.

"Let's go out and show Millie the barn and the carriage house and our play places," said Bert. "Frank and I have got a trapeze, Joe fixed it for us. We're goin' to learn to swing by our feet." And he danced up and down in excitement.

Josie wanted to show her the house first, but Bert put in scornfully. "The house! Pooh! She can see the house any ole time. She lives in a house in Boston, don't she? But I bet she hasn't got a barn where she lives – have you Millie?"

"N-no," Millie acknowledged, "Nor a trapeze either. My papa took me to a circus last summer, though, and I saw some ladies and men on trapezes a-way up in the air, and one man threw the ladies by their feet a-way across the tent and the other man would catch them by their hands or their feet! My goodness, I was scared! Maybe we can learn to do that too! Let's go out and see the barn first, Josie, and we can look at the house tomorrow."

Josie, who was always good natured, agreed, although she was secretly wondering if Millie hadn't been fibbing a little about the circus and women flying through the air! Bert was a little skeptical too, and later repeated the tale to Joe, who promptly told him it was probably quite true.

They scampered across to the barn and explored it thoroughly, the grain room, horse stall, cow tie-up, and finally, up the straight ladder to the hay loft. There Millie soon learned the delight of jumping from the beams into the mass of soft, sweet smelling hay. Bert was somewhat taken back at her prowess in that line, for even though it was entirely new to her, she was a game little girl and took jump for jump after him, although he had expected to be a soloist when it came to the higher beam. Josie jumped too, from the lower one, but balked at going any higher.

Then suddenly Bert started looking in all the corners and poking about generally, until Millie's curiosity was aroused.

"What you lookin' for, Bert?" she queried.

"Eggs," he replied, briefly. "Eggs?" she repeated. "I saw a hen house and lots of hens down in the field. Why don't you look down there for your eggs?"

"Oh, *those* are mama's eggs. But lots of times the hens steal up here in the hay, and mama lets us have all we find."

Still puzzled, Millie went on. "Bert, what do you *want* of 'em –do you eat 'em?" and she wrinkled up her nose, for she wasn't particularly fond of eggs herself.

The other two laughed, and Bert answered, "No, silly. Mama lets us take 'em up to Parker's store, an' we get sump'n for 'em, - candy maybe, or p'haps a box of crayons, or fish hooks. I'm goin' to get some hooks this time."

Millie frowned in utter perplexity. "Candy," she repeated, "candy, or crayons, or fish hooks – for *eggs*! Don't you have to pay *money* for things at Parker's store?"

Bert hooted, and Josie laughed again, but tried to explain the financing. "Well, eggs are the same as money," she said instructively. "A cent apiece, so if we take five eggs, we can get five cent's worth of candy, or whatever we want. One time we had twelve eggs at once, - twelve cents! We found three nests that day."

Millie still looked slightly bewildered, and remarked quite reasonably- "Well, I should think it would be lots easier to just ask you mama for five cents, than to poke around all over this barn looking for eggs!"

"Yes, I guess it would," replied Josie, "Only she doesn't have many nickels to spare for candy, so she lets us have the eggs. She says it's better to *earn* spendin' money, anyway."

"Sometimes we find 'em in the carriage house too," put in Bert. "I found three once, right up on the seat of the new surrey!"

"Yes, an' once he found a nest right out in the middle of the rhubarb bed," Josie said. "He mos' stepped on 'em, -an' it had nine eggs in it! Mama opened those for cooking though, cause she was afraid some of 'em would be bad, an' Mr. Parker wouldn't like *that* I can tell you!"

"An' were they bad?" Millie inquired, deeply interested.

"Only three of 'em. So mama gave us six cents."

Millie reviewed the matter silently for a few moments, and then said generously, "well, I'll help you hunt every day so you can get lots of pennies."

But Josie and Bert could be generous too, and Josie replied, with Bert nodding affirmatively, "You can hunt with us Millie, if you want to, but you can have the pennies yourself for those you find."

"We'll hunt harder," Bert added. "Maybe you'll find five or six before Friday. We most always go up to the village Fridays, 'cause mama shops for Sunday and the next week."

"All right," Millie exclaimed, hopping up and down and clapping her hands. "But if we don't find any I'll get some candy anyway," she added, while the others stared at such a reckless statement.

"You got money for candy?" Bert asked, respectfully.

"Uh huh. My papa gives me ten cents every Saturday. He says that's my 'lowance, and then if I've been a good girl, he buys me a ten cent box of ice-cream at Kelley's on our corner. I most always get choc'late."

Her companions were speechless at such prodigality, but Millie went on calmly. "He gave me a quarter this morning when he left mama and me at the train, for popcorn or sumpin'. But I didn't get any cause I was too busy lookin' out the window. An' I've got my ten cents from last Saturday too. Maybe we can get some ice-cream Friday. Does Mr. Parker sell ice-cream?"

Recovering their speech after a stunned silence at such unparalleled wealth, they explained that Parker's sold just about everything except ice-cream, but hastily added that it could be had at Otis Sumner's Drug Store just across the river.

"But its five cents a scoop," warned Bert.

"And ten cents for a plate full," added Josie.

"That's all right," returned Millie, grandly. "We'll have a scoop each, anyway, maybe a plate, but anyway a scoop and candy. I'll get another ten cents Saturday anyhow."

Once more there was a short period of silence while her listeners had mental visions of going into Sumner's, sitting down at one of the little tables, and ordering ice-cream, possibly a plateful! – AND for cash money too – not EGGS! They wondered if Millie's father was one of those millionaires, which would have amused him mightily, had he known it.

But presently they resumed the search for eggs, more ardently than ever, and were rewarded by finding three nests, one with three eggs, one with two, and the last with just one. Bert had found two nests and Josie the other, - and a new phase of the egg business struck Millie.

"Are these *your* eggs, Josie, or Bert's?"

"Oh, we have our own basket out in the buttery, and half are mine and half his- anyway."

"But 'sposin' he found most of 'em?" Millie asked, curious about such an arrangement.

"We both *look* – so mama says half each is a fair thing," and Millie was satisfied.

After the eggs were safely deposited in their basket, the children resumed their tour of inspection.

In the carriage house there was a swing hung from the rafters, for rainy days, Bert explained, for there was one at the side of the house, as well as a hammock. There were several work carts, and a beautiful surrey, its top adorned with wide cream-colored fringe. Millie admired it immensely and climbed in at once.

"We go for rides sometimes, when papa is home," said Josie, following her and seating herself beside Millie in the back seat.

"He lets me drive, too, sometimes," said Bert who had climbed into the front seat. He cracked the whip expertly, and added, "maybe he'll let you sometime – after you've learned to drive."

"Pooh!" exclaimed Millie scornfully, "I know how to drive *now*."

"You do not!" contradicted Bert.

"I do so! That man – I forget his name, - that man that brought mama and me from the train – he let me drive clear to the corner, so there, Bert Paige!"

"Ho! Ho!" sneered Bert, "you only held the reins, I bet! I bet you never drove a horse in your life!"

"We-ll,- I did so drive today, anyway. That man......."

Josie broke in, trying to avert a quarrel, like the little peacemaker she was. "He's Joe Gilmore. He lets me hold the reins too, and I play I'm really driving. Papa says he'll teach me next time we go to ride, and I know he'll teach you too."

Millie's scowl vanished and the angry red in her cheeks died down, while Bert hung his head feeling very uncomfortable, because he realized he had been rude to their new friend.

"Where's your horse?" Millie asked after a moment's silence. "Is he white like Joe's horse?"

"No" replied Bert, answering the last question first. "He's gray with darker spots, an' he's handsomer than ole Samson. He's over in the back pasture with the cows an' his name is "Gasus.""

"That's a funny name, isn't it?" exclaimed Millie.

"Tisn't "Gasus," Josie put in, laughing "It's Pegasus. Bert never says it right!"

Millie couldn't see that there was much choice between the two names, but made no further remarks, and Josie went on. "Come on; let's go over to the pasture and see him. "I'll take him some carrots."

"How long will it take to cook them" asked Millie, innocently, and Bert almost forgot himself and was rude again, but he caught Josie's admonishing eye, and merely grinned at such colossal ignorance.

"Don't have to cook 'em," he said simply. "He likes 'em raw." So, being thoroughly informed as to horses and carrots, she started off for further exploration.

Just to the right of the carriage house door lay a huge boulder, as high as the eaves, and almost as big as the carriage house itself, and here Josie stopped. "That's Big Rock," she said, "an' it's my favoritest play place. See, it slants here in front, and you can walk right up to the top," she added, suiting the action to the word. "It's nice and flat up here, an' I play here a lot."

A gnarled and misshapen apple tree grew close beside it, giving a nice shade, and Bert immediately climbed into it from the top of the rock. A large limb had rotted away and dropped off, leaving a good sized hole, which Josie pointed to, and calmly declared to be a snake hole. "least I *think* it is," she said. "It looks like it would be a good place for a snake to live in."

Millie looked at it, and backed away swiftly. "Won't it come out an' sting you?" She questioned fearfully.

Bert looked at her a moment, and seeing she was serious, he proceeded to enlighten her further. "Naw, 'course it won't. Snakes are scareder of people than people are of snakes! Sides, snakes don't *sting*, they BITE!"

Millie thought she would as soon be stung as bitten, but she accepted his statement with a subdued "Oh!" And she peered fearfully into the hole. But no snake appeared, for which she was duly thankful. But, even with a snake hole at such close quarters, she agreed with Josie that the rock was a wonderful place to play. She did not dream then, how many years it would prove to be so, or how many "secrets" she and Josie would share, or how many escapades she and Bert would "hatch up" on the rough gray boulder.

After a while they sauntered down a wood road behind the barn, across a little rise of ledges, stopping to pick and eat a few early raspberries, growing along the stone wall. But when they reached the top of the rise, Millie gave a squeal of delight, for at the foot, on the other side; a little brook rippled and gurgled. Just a tiny brook, for Bert had made a dam of stones and bits of wood, so that off to the right it had widened into a small pool. The ledges led straight into this for several feet, making a perfect place to paddle, clean and white and solid underfoot. Beyond it, the water looked black and muddy, and very uninviting.

In no time at all, Bert and Josie were splashing away, for both were barefooted. Millie stood for a moment, watching them enviously, and then plumped herself down and began pulling off her little black pumps and white stockings. And in about ten seconds flat, she too was paddling happily, and trying to catch the tiny tadpoles and minnows that darted in every direction.

But after a while, Bert said it must be about time to get the cows and Pegasus, so the girls left the brook reluctantly, and even more reluctantly Millie picked up her shoes and stockings. She had instantly and whole heartedly been converted to a barefoot existence, declaring she would keep them off.

"You'll hurt your feet *awful* if you do," Bert declared. "It's awful stony on the path to the back pasture. Put your shoes on anyhow, an' start goin' barefoot tomorrow, round the yard, till you get your feet toughened up." And she very wisely followed his advice.

When they reached the pasture bars Bert let them down and said, "I'll go drive 'em up. Josie, you stand over that side, an' Millie, you over there, then they won't go maugin' off into the bushes." He went off calling loudly, "CO-BOSS, CO- BOSS," and almost immediately two Jersey cows came ambling into sight. They were fat and handsome, and great pets, but to Millie, unused to cows, they looked enormous and ferocious, so that when one of them branched toward her, she was over the stone wall and racing toward Bert, who stared at her in disgust.

"Fraidy cat!" he jeered. "Fraid of an ole cow! Pooh, they wouldn't hurt a flea," and then he added loftily, "You just better get over bein' afraid of every little thing if you're goin' to be round ME! I'll look out for you. Come on," and he stalked ahead, followed meekly by a much taken down young lady.

She even contrived to appear unconcerned when she discovered that a huge gray horse was winding up the procession – not more than ten feet behind her! But she was mightily relieved just the same, when Josie fell back and joined her, giving the horse a pat and a carrot. Nevertheless, she was careful to keep in front of Josie and behind Bert, so she felt comparatively safe. I'm glad to say that under Bert's protection, she soon became use to animals, both wild and domestic, - even snakes became a matter of indifference to her.

When they reached the barnyard, Bert watered the three animals, and they drifted up the ramp and to their places in the barn. Whereupon Bert heaved a deep sigh, and said forcefully – "There! Thank goodness THOSE chores are done!"

"Chores? What are chores??" Questioned Millie, interestedly.

Bert stared at her blankly, but Josie laughed and said briefly, "Work."

"Work?" Millie repeated.

"Sure. Anything you *have* to do is work and anything that is work is a chore, - see? Bert has to bring up the cows and water 'em, so that's one of his chores."

"Two of 'em, you mean," Bert interposed.

Millie pondered over the matter a moment, and then asked, "Well, do you have to do it too?"

"N-no," replied Josie, "I don't *have* to, but I most always *do* go with him. I like to, 'cause we most always stop to paddle in the brook." Then with a deep sigh she added. "Helping with the dishes in one of my chores."

"Yes." Bert put in, "and I have to keep the wood box filled, an' chop up kindling, an' drive the cows over to the pasture mornins' - - seems to me I have an *awful* lot of chores to do!" and he added a sigh to Josie's.

Millie added a third sigh, and said, "Well, I guess I have chores to do too, only I didn't know you called 'em that. Mama calls 'em 'stints'. "Come an' do your stint, Millie," she mimicked so perfectly that although the others did not know her mother very well, they recognized the voice, and laughed uproariously. "I have to do a quilt square ev'ry single day 'cept Sundays," she went on, and sighed again.

"That ain't *work* tho'," said Bert disparagingly.

"It is too," snapped Millie. "I hate that kind of sewing, an' if I don't do it good, Mama just rips it out an' I have to do it all over again! I don't mind sewing for my dollies, tho, and I kinda *like* to 'broider.'"

"Broider?" repeated Josie. "What's broider?"

"Oh, broidery, - well, it's kinda like sewing, only you make pictures on a piece of cloth. I'm makin' a splasher for my Grammy's Christmas present. It's outline stitch an' it's birds takin' a bath. They're red – in t-tambo cotton. It's real pretty. I'll show it to you tomorrow."

They both looked at their new friend with deep respect. Certainly making pictures of birds, with red t-tambo cotton, whatever that was, was quite as much of a chore as filling wood boxes or helping with dishes.

They crossed the road and found their mothers sitting under the maples, getting acquainted and they sat down on the grass with Jennie, who was playing with her blocks and toys.

Presently, Aunt Ella left to milk, and a little later there was supper to be eaten, and afterwards a quiet half hour sitting on the big door rock, watching the sun go down behind the barn. And then Aunt Nellie observed that Millie was half asleep, and she too felt tired and drowsy, so 'good-nights' were said, and they were soon upstairs in the South chamber, getting ready for bed.

Millie had finished her prayers and was tucked in on her side of the big bed, when she suddenly remarked, "Mama, I like this best of any place I was ever in!"

"What, the bed?" asked her mother, surprised.

"No, course not! I mean here, 'stead of Boston. I wish I never had to go back to Boston."

"Why Millie! And never see papa again?"

"Course not," Millie exclaimed vehemently, sitting up straight at such an idea. "I mean I wish we could all stay here. I bet papa will like it here, too, an' maybe he'll want to stay here." She sank back to her pillow, and after a moment went on, sleepily, "I'm goin' to help Josie an' Bert do their chores tomorrow, an' then we'll have more time to play. An' tomorrow I'm goin' barefooted – I can, can't I, Mama?"

But she didn't even hear her mother's "I guess so, dear," - for she was fast asleep.

For a moment her mother watched her, wondering what she had meant by "chores", but too sleepy herself to ponder on it very long.

And so ended their first day in Goffstown. Millie was only "half past six" but she has never forgotten that first, wonderful, happy day. Nor has her allegiance ever wavered (altho' she is now long past seventy year's old) (written in 1960)

Chapter III

The days that followed were filled with one joyous time after another, from early morning till dusk, but first, of course, Millie had to be shown every nook and cranny of the old house.

It was really much larger than it had appeared to be, for there were two ells, one running back parallel with the Centre Road, and one off the south side, which was really a shed.

At the right of the front door was the sitting room, as living rooms were called in those days - a pleasant room with windows fronting the road and the South, showing the mountains across the river. In one of these stood the sewing machine, piled high with mending This, however, rapidly diminished for Aunt Nellie loved to sew and mend, and was adept with the needle, and as Millie said, she took this mending as her "chore."

On the other side of the hall was the "parlor," – seldom used, being sacred to special, very special occasions. Josie showed this room with such admiration and pride, that Millie was much impressed and awed.

There was a deep green carpet lavishly adorned with huge red roses, and four windows, whose shades were carefully drawn behind long Nottingham drapes, lest the sun fade the lovely roses.

On the walls hung life-size crayon portraits of dead and gone Paiges, and an oil painting, done by Aunt Ella when in high school. There were three chairs and a sofa, with beautifully curved backs, upholstered in green rep, a Boston Rocker, and between the two front windows, a walnut, marble topped table. In its center stood a glass case protecting a gorgeous bouquet of wax flowers, on one side the big family Bible, and on the other a plush family album. And there was also, to Millie, the most wonderful thing she had ever seen, a Stereoscope, with its case of photographs. She never tired of looking through it, although most of the pictures were of gory scenes of battles in the Civil War. And she never understood why *two* scenes on each photograph, should only appear once, much enlarged, when looked at through the lens of the Stereoscope!

And lastly, in one corner of the room, was a walnut "What Not," its shelves loaded with the most interesting things – figurines, curios of all kinds, a crystal ball which produced a most realistic snow storm when turned upside down, and a bottle, quite small, but containing a good sized ship in full sail! It certainly was a wonderful room, and the children often slipped in to sit quietly, sometimes looking at the various things, sometimes just admiring.

Upstairs there were two bedrooms, the North and South Chambers, low posted and with eaves nearly to the floor. Millie and her Mother occupied the South room and Josie the other. To Millie's delight, in a few days after their arrival, she was given permission to share Josie's room with her, and how she loved it! She loved the high, old fashioned bedstead with it's painted head and foot boards, and the fat, deep featherbed, so soft and comfortable, and for many summers the two girls enjoyed the room together.

Back of the sitting room was the immense dining room with its long table capable of seating ten or twelve without the extra leaves. There was a fascinating 'Secretary' in one corner, full of books and papers, and in the opposite corner, a huge iron range, for in winter this room was used as a combination dining room and kitchen.

Bert's room led from this to the left, and was back of the parlor. It was a typical boy's room, with books, curious bits of rocks, bird's eggs, a fishing pole, and on one wall, his greatest treasure, a real sword, that had been through the Civil War.

A pantry also led from the dining room, connecting it with the North, or summer kitchen and back of this were two bedrooms, Aunt Ella's and a 'spare room.'

From the end of the dining room there was a back hall and side door, and across this hall was the Buttery. Millie had never heard of a Buttery, but this one visit to it convinced her that it was about the best place in the whole house! There were tall cupboards whose doors were of cheese cloth instead of wood, and whose shelves were loaded with crocks and jars full of cookies and cakes and doughnuts. There was a tall rack for pies – six or seven always, sometimes more, all luscious and inviting. And jars of jellies and jams, honey and maple syrup - oh, the Buttery was a lovely, sweet smelling place I assure you!

Four steps led down from it to the shed, which was also a 'smelly' place, though not at all inviting, for in the corner was a big barrel into which all the sour milk and table scraps were kept for the pigs. Millie and Josie always wrinkled their noses when they passed it, and were glad that "feedin' the pigs" was one of Bert's chores, and not theirs! There were chopping blocks, and piles of chips for kindling fires, and row upon row of stove wood, neatly piled, and almost reaching the rafters.

A door led to the lawn, and at once Millie noticed the oblong cut from it. "What's that hole for?" she asked, and Josie replied that they had had a dog, and the hole was cut so he could go in and out when he pleased. "He was a lovely dog," she said, "but he died last spring. I cried awf'ly and so did Mama, but Papa's got another – soon as it's old enough to leave it's mother. I used to get in and out through there, but I can't now, I'm too fat." And she laughed with Millie.

"I bet I can," said the latter, and promptly demonstrated that she could, with room to spare.

Beyond this shed was a sort of tool room, and at the very end of that was a small room, not over six feet square. Against one wall, under a small window, was a sort of bench, with three very neat ovals cut out, each with a board cover. Millie had been escorted to this room shortly after her arrival, when she had stated briefly, "I want to go to the bath room." She had thought it the queerest "bath room" she had ever seen, but became accustomed to it after a few days, and stopped groping for the 'string to pull!' In fact, it became a sort of club room to the two girls, who often retired to it to tell secrets - knowing it to be safe from intrusion if the door was closed. They never seemed to tire of studying the pictures and old calendars that bedecked the walls, or of poring over the old catalogs in the box of corn cobs in the corner.

The attic proved a fascinating place too, full of trunks and boxes filled with clothing or books, or things that had been hoarded for years. They spent many a rainy day up there, playing 'grown-up,' attiring themselves in old dresses, coats and hats, relics of past days.

Once the house was thoroughly inspected, Josie and Bert took it upon themselves to introduce her to the neighbors. She liked old Mrs. Little, who, although a semi-invalid loved to have them call on her, and "Walker," her husband too. At first his sober and rather taciturn manner rather awed the little Boston girl, but she soon discovered the twinkle in his blue eyes and that he liked young folks, so they were soon on excellent terms. And she immediately liked Jim Hazeltine, who lived with them, and helped with the farm work. Jim wasn't considered 'exactly bright,' but never-the-less he was smart and shrewd in many ways, a good farmer and judge of livestock.

She liked the Gilmores, Joe's parents, too, and the Tewksburys and Moores, in the house beyond. And she liked Frank Underhill and his parents, having forgiven him for his insult the day she arrived! At Pecoy's, she found Mabel a congenial soul, as big a tomboy as she was herself, and for many years the two were often rivals in games and stunts.

But she found calling on the Phillips' the most delightful of all. There was a wonderful swing in the front yard, and always, it seemed, a new litter of kittens. There was the most gorgeous flower bed, which always yielded big bouquets to take home to their mothers. Emma, their daughter, about eleven, was shy and quiet, but always ready to push them in the swing, or show them her dolls and toys. Maybe, best of all, was the fact that Mrs. Phillips always had a little tea party, with delicious cakes and tarts or cookies, and *tea*! Of course it was Cambric tea, but hot, and with thick cream and lots of sugar. It made them feel quite grown up, I assure you.

And there was Blanche Whipple, and down the Centre road the three Davis boys. Oh, yes, Millie liked the Paige Hill neighbors, one and all.

Perhaps, after she had played some of her pranks, some of the older neighbors thought of her as 'that pestiferous young one from Boston,' but they grew used to her after a while, and realized that she wasn't really naughty, 'jest full of it,' as Uncle David said.

So, now that she has met them all, we will leave her, and try and tell about some of the good times she and her companions had that first wonderful summer.

Chapter IV

One hot, sunny afternoon, Bert lay sprawled flat on his back on the grass, while Millie and Josie sat on the door rock in the shade of the lilac clump, puffing and panting after a long and hard game of tag.

Josie's eyes seemed to be fixed on the big Balm of Gilead tree that towered over the barn across the road and suddenly, having regained her breath, she jumped to her feet, exclaiming. "I know what's let's do. Let's play keeping shop. I'll be a dress- maker and Millie, you can be a milliner an' we'll make dresses an' hats. An' Bert can play he's a rich man an' come to the shop an' buy things for his wife."

"I will *not*," Bert flatly declared. "That's a silly ole girl's game, an' I won't buy dresses an' hats for my wife, 'cause I haven't got one. I wouldn't have a wife if you *paid* me." He went on emphatically. "Goodness sakes, let's play somethin' sides *that* kind of game. Come on out to the barn an' play circus."

But Josie was tired from running and refused, and Millie, interested in her proposition, also refused.

Bert, in indignation, muttered darkly, "all right for you! Go ahead an' play dressmakers and what-you-call-ems! I'm goin' down to Frank's an' play circus so there." He stalked off in a very dignified manner as he crossed the lawn, but broke into a gallop when he reached the road, yelling at the top of his voice, "GIT AP ' – GO ALONG THERE OLE HORSE. GIT AP, I TELL YOU!" Evidently he was starting his circus career right then and there.

Millie was tempted to tear after him, having visions of herself as a beautiful equestrian in a bespangled tulle skirt, riding a snow white horse. But, after all, playing circus was an old story, while this dress and hat business was something new, and she was always willing to investigate new ideas.

"What you goin' to make 'em of Josie?" She questioned, after Bert was out of hearing.

"Wait a minute," Josie replied, and ran into the house to return in a few moments with their round pointed scissors. "Come on," she said, and led the way to the Balm of Gilead tree. A regular jungle of young shoots grew thickly all round the great trunk, and to Millie's surprise, Josie began snipping off their big, shiny leaves, instructing her pupil to do the same.

"What you want all these old leaves for?" she asked, obeying the order, but still puzzled.

"Why, to make the skirts an' hats of. I'll show you how. I've played it lots of times, only it isn't much fun alone, an' Bert won't *ever* play it with me.

So they worked away industriously, until they had quite a pile of leaves. "Now I'll show you how to make a hat,' Josie began instructively, as they sat down in the shade. "Hats are easier to make then skirts, and don't take so long to make either."

She snipped the stems off close to the leaves, and started with one leaf, as a center, she overlapped another, fastening it by using the stems as a pin, and so on round and round.

Millie watched intently, wriggling with excitement as she saw the circlet growing larger and larger. Finally she could stand it no longer, and seizing leaves and stems, she started one of her own. "No, Millie, not that way," interposed her instructress. "If you pin 'em so close to the edges, they'll tear right out. Lap them way over, - see? Like this. It takes longer, but they won't tear."

When Josie's circlet was done she placed it on her head, posed gracefully, and said. "There! Doesn't that make a pretty hat?" And Millie nodded admiringly. Presently hers was done too, and they strutted round for a while, until Josie said, "Now we'll play store. You make one or two more hats an' I'll start a skirt. It takes quite a while to make a skirt, 'cause they rip so easy. After you get some made, I'll come along an' buy one. Maybe I'll buy two, one for Sundays, an' one for week days."

So for awhile, the two sat quietly, busy as beavers. Josie was so intent on her skirt, that she did not notice that Millie got up several times and wandered about nearby. By and by she said impatiently, "Oh dear, I can't make this ole skirt stay together! It keeps tearing apart. I guess I'll make some hats instead." And then she gave a surprised squeal as she saw Millie's hats lying beside her. She picked one up and squealed again, for really it was quite a confection! Having them all alike, just plain circlets had not satisfied Millie's artistic sense. On the side of one she had pinned a half circle of yellow Tansy blossoms, on another a cluster of the various wild grasses that grew all about the place, and a third she had turned up on one side and fastened with a bunch of tiny wild flowers. It really was very dashing and rather rakish.

Josie was much excited over these creations, and tried them all on, one after the other. "Why, Miss Rumney!" She exclaimed stepping gracefully into the role of buyer. "What beautiful hats you do make! I never thought of putting trimming on them. I just *love* this one with the blue flowers! I guess I'll buy it for Sunday. How much is it?"

Millie's face fell, for she liked it best, too, but she took the part of milliner as readily as Josie had that of customer, and replied, 'I'm very sorry, Miss Paige, but *that* one isn't for sale. I made that one for myself. You could have this one with the green feathers, though, "and she held out the grass trimmed hat.

But when she saw Josie's disappointed face, her good heart prevailed, and she went on, hastily, "Oh well, I guess you can have it if you want it. I can make another for myself by and by. It is quite es'pensive though – fifty cents!" She wondered if "Miss Paige" would pay so exorbitant a price, but she did, with no hesitation whatever, and donning the hat again, sat down to resume work on the troublesome skirt.

Hats wilted and the skirt kept tearing apart, but they doggedly stuck to it, two patient little workers. They were rewarded, too, for Aunt Ella passed on her way to the hen house, and seeing their difficulty, explained that it was the weight of so many leaves that caused the trouble. "I'll tell you what," she said, "Millie, you run into the house and get a paper of pins from the top machine drawer, and Josie, you skip into the grain room and get a couple of meal sacks. Cut the bottoms off, and pin the leaves to the sacks, with real pins. I think they will hold all right."

Off they dashed on their errands, - and – sure enough, the skirts turned out successfully. All the rest of the afternoon they strutted around, called on Aunt Nellie, who was resting in the hammock, and had a happy time till called in to supper.

On other days, perhaps they would play Doctor, Nurse and patient, Bert enacting old Dr. George to the life. Usually Josie played Nurse, and if Jennie could be coaxed into being the patient, which was seldom Millie would be her heartbroken mother. At other times, she would be the patient and her pains, aches and sufferings were so realistically portrayed that sometimes she scared Josie into real tears!

Some days Bert demanded more strenuous games, cowboys, bandits or Indians. These usually called for Frank, and were decidedly popular. Oftenest it was Indians, and by request from the older members of the family, was usually played over on the ledges by the brook. Bert liked to be chief, and had made a head piece from an old belt and hen feathers. With this war-bonnet, and his face painted with choke cherry or blackberry juice, he really was a ferocious looking red man!

They had made tents of grain bags and pine boughs and had raids, wars, scalpings, tomahawking and war dances. Millie usually led the war dances, squaw though she was, for she had seen real wild west shows and could let out war whoop's and ululation's that nearly deafened the others.

Now and then they went to the other extreme and played "Church," with Millie as the minister generally, for none of the others wanted to preach sermons. Her attire had greatly puzzled Frank, Bert and Josie, for none of them had ever seen an Episcopal minister in his robes. But Bert was the only one who criticized or expressed himself. Upon asking what that white thing was, and being told it was a surplice, he had sniffed scornfully and said, "Taint neither a surplice! It's one of mama's nightgowns!" They held weddings, marrying their dolls, and funerals, burying dead chickens, or birds or what have you! Sometimes the minister's eulogies at the latter sad rites were truly heart-rending!

Sometimes it was Drug Store, and they ransacked the house from attic to cellar for empty bottles, cartons and boxes. They served delicious soda, made from water, vinegar, a drop of vanilla and soda – and it really fizzed! They colored water with ink, bluing, berry juices – anything they could get hold of, and sand made splendid powders of all kinds.

Often, it was school, usually with Josie as teacher. If Bert did not play, and Jennie (and in later years, Flora and Florence) did, then Millie would be a "good" scholar, studious and obedient. But when Bert could be induced to play – what a change! It became a race to see which of the two could be the most recalcitrant, disobedient, stupid pupil! They were incorrigible, *very* naughty children, and being stood in corners, made to wear dunce caps, kept after school or sent home with notes to their parents, failed to improve their conduct in the least! Poor Miss Paige had a hard time of it with two such trials in her class.

There had been afternoons at the river, paddling or playing in the sand, or collecting pretty stones. And afternoons of berrying, and of course, they went over to the brook nearly every day.

They did not always play alone, for on many days, children in the neighborhood came to play with them, or they would visit them at their homes. And there were visits to the Village with treats of ice cream or soda or to the Centre to the little store there. So the days went flying past, full of fun and play, and some "chores" of course.

Millie had never been so happy in all her life before, and although her mother sometimes wondered how she stood so much activity, it was quite evident that she was thriving on it! So she was allowed to romp along, without many "stints" or "chores" or very much discipline. As Dr. Street had put it, she was allowed to "run loose."

Chapter V

One lovely morning in early August the children were in deep debate all through breakfast, as to what they would do that day, when Aunt Ella settled the matter by saying briskly, "Now you children stay right in the yard this morning, and don't go scampering off."

Of course there was a chorus of expostulations, "Why, Mama?" "Why not, Mama??" and "What can we do just staying in the yard?" When she could make herself heard again she replied, "Well, I thought maybe we would have a picnic today." Whereupon there was a right about face and another chorus, this time one of unanimous assent. "Goodie, oh goodie!" they shouted, until even baby Jennie caught the excitement and banging her mug on her high chair, shouted, "Doody, doody!" till she was red in the face.

"Where we goin' to have it Mama?" asked Josie, after quiet had been restored, and Bert cried, "Down to the river – let's go down to the river!" Millie was too excited to say a word, but waited expectantly for the decision. This was the first time a real all day picnic had been suggested, and she was thinking that if it was half as much fun as the other joys of Paige Hill, she was for it 100%.

"Well," Aunt Ella finally replied, busy clearing off the breakfast table, "We can go to the river I suppose, but I was thinking it would be nice to go down to Harry Brook."

There was another shout and prancing about by Bert and Josie, who exclaimed, "Oh yes, Mama! Millie hasn't been down there either! There's such lots of lovely places to play, and it's lots more fun swimming down there, than at the river!"

"That's right," agreed Bert. "Golly, I know a dandy place down there – it's awful deep, a pool down the brook just a little ways."

Aunt Nellie instantly began to look worried, but before Aunt Ella could reassure her, Bert continued, "It's a big pool, ' bout half as big as this room, an' out in the middle it's awful deep – most up to my waist!" Aunt Nellie breathed a sigh of relief, knowing it couldn't be very dangerous!

Millie was still speechless with joy! A picnic! A brook! With a pool as deep as that! Why, maybe she could learn to really swim, - big as half the dining room! And with that thought she recovered her speech, and chattered like a magpie, dancing round like a whirling dervish.

In the meantime, Aunt Ella had been assuring Millie's mother as to the safety of Harry Brook. "That's the deepest it is, ever, and it won't be that deep after this spell of dry weather. I don't like to have them go in at the river unless some of the men folks are round, for there are a few deep holes. So I proposed the brook."

Turning to the children, she went on. "Now then, scamper and get your chores done and Bert, when you come in from the barn, bring your express wagon please, as we'll need it. Oh, and by the way, young man, please be sure and fill the wood box today, not just cover the bottom as you did yesterday!"

"I will Mama," promised Bert, looking rather sheepish. "I meant to come right back yesterday and fill it, but I ran down to Frank's about our new camp, and forgot all about it!" And then, a sudden thought striking him, he went on "Mama, can't I ask Frank to go with us today?"

"Why, of course," she assented, for Frank was rather a lonely little boy when Bert was away. The neighborhood seemed to be surfeited with girls, but shy on boys!

"You may run down and ask him *after* your chores are all done," and then she added hastily, for he was half way to the door, "And Bert, be *sure* to tell Helen not to bother with any lunch, for I've plenty for everybody, all put up."

Bert flew for the barn, and his mother turned to the others. "Now then, Josie, you hyper and get the dishes stacked up all ready for me to wash and you may wipe them. Then make your bed, for we want to make an early start."

Josie willingly "hypered," and so did Millie, for her mother had told her to help Josie with the dishes and making their beds.

So everybody got busy, and "in two shakes of a lamb's tail," as Josie said, dishes were out of the way, the table set and the big white mosquito netting spread over it, beds were made and the house in "apple pie order."

Aunt Nellie had been helping put up the lunch in the big basket and various boxes, and had exclaimed at the quantity of food. But Aunt Ella only laughed and said, "My goodness, Nellie, you don't know what appetites children have at a picnic! There'll be precious little to bring back I can tell you!" Which afterwards proved to be quite true.

At last everything was ready, and Bert was back with Frank. They loaded the basket and boxes into the express wagon, which Bert was to pull as far as the last bars. Then the things were to be distributed for carrying, so that Jennie could ride the rest of the way. The pasture roads ended there and the balance of the way was too rough and stony for such a little girl. Frank carried a stone jug filled with the children's favorite drink. Molasses, ginger and water, and Aunt Nellie another one filled with good cold water from the well. Aunt Ella carried a large box very carefully, although no one knew what was in it, and Josie and Millie each had hold of one of Jennie's hands.

They sang, and laughed, and chatted merrily, and waved to Mrs. Moore and Alice who were picking berries, as they went through the Moore pasture. Then came another pasture, and then the bars that opened in the "McCoy Place," where they were to picnic. Here the contents of the cart were divided, and Jennie seated in it, riding in state, laughing and squealing at the bumps and "thank you marms."

It was a long walk and a rough one, down hill most of the way, but no one minded. They passed through a grove of huge chestnut trees, and the children had to pick their way carefully, to avoid the sharp brown burrs, for, of course, they were barefooted, as usual. By this time, Millie's feet had become almost as tough as the others, but Aunt Nellie still fussed every night, about the stubbed toes and bruises.

After a while, they reached the bottom of the down grade, and after a short walk on level ground, Millie saw an old dilapidated house, with the paint almost entirely peeled off, and a small barn, almost falling apart, which had never been painted at all. A jungle of wild rose and raspberry bushes filled the space between them, but of course it was too late for roses, and there were few berries.

Once on the flat ground, Jennie had scrambled from the cart, and followed the other children who were racing for the brook with shouts and whoops. The two grown-ups found a shady place under a cluster of trees, and thankfully sat down to get a breath and rest a while.

The boys had worn old linen pants, so they required no bathing suits, - simply dropped off their blouses and were in the brook in about one minute flat! Millie and Josie had carried old dresses, for children seldom had bathing suits in those days. A moment or two in the bushes and out they popped, and IN they popped. There was much squealing for the water seemed cold after their long hot walk.

Aunt Nellie jumped up, feeling that she must hold on to Millie's skirts, or at least be close at hand, but seeing that Aunt Ella sat placid and unconcerned, and that the water barely reached the children's knees, she relaxed. She wished she had Ella's calm nerves, when she saw that she did not interfere, even when Jennie paddled in, all dressed though she was. The two older girls held out their hands and told her to come along – which she proceeded to do, lost her balance, and PLOP! Down she sat with a splash! For a second, she looked startled, but when everyone laughed, even her Mother, she laughed too, and shouted, "Me fall down! Dot my botty all wet!" and slapped at the water with both hands until she was wet from head to foot!

The rest of the forenoon the five children frolicked round the brook, now in and now out of it, or raced about the flat, picking flowers, or a few late blueberries or blackberries.

They peeked between the planks of the old barn, but there was little to be seen except a pile of dusty hay and the remains of an old hay rack in one corner. And peeking under the torn red window shade of the one window of the old house yielded nothing much either – just a glimpse of an old rusty stove and a broken chair. A few years later, however, they were to find (they thought) a mystery in the old house! But that belongs to another chapter and will have to wait.

In the meantime, as they sat sewing and mending under the trees, Aunt Ella was telling what she could of the history of the forlorn looking old place.

Originally, though long ago, a road from the Centre had run directly in front of the house, connecting with the village road just above Paige's. But later, the town discarded it, for there were no other farms on it, and they refused the up-keep of it. So it had grown up to weeds and brush until one could hardly believe there had ever been a road at all, and the old house was left desolate and alone in the middle of fields and pastures.

But it had been home to old Mr. McCoy and he had loved it, and refused to move away. Later, his daughter, Rhodica Hazeltine, and her little boy Jimmie, came to live with him, and after a while he became ill and died.

It was the custom, in those days, for the men in a neighborhood to take turns staying nights where there was serious illness, and the Paige boys had done so, even David, who was only thirteen. There were no real undertakers either. Old John Whipple attended to all such duties in that vicinity.

It happened that Mr. McCoy had died on one of the nights David was staying, so he was obliged to walk, all alone, up through the pastures, to have one of his older brothers go after Mr. Whipple. It was a long, cold and lonely walk for the boy, although he remembers minding the loneliness and darkness more than the cold or distance.

Jimmie and his mother stayed on in the old house. They were quite poor, and she earned a living for them both by helping at the farms round about, cooking, washing and cleaning. Jimmie was too small to be left alone so he went with her, trudging the long way up and back when her day's work was done. Oftenest she worked at the Little farm, for Mrs. Little had never been very well, and could do very little work herself.

Mrs. Hazeltine had been a very brave woman, and it was well she was, for it required courage to live so far from neighbors. She proved it one cold, foggy fall night, for when she and Jimmie reached the flat that led to the house, they saw a large white figure wandering slowly about the yard.

Little Jimmie was badly frightened, and clung to his mother's skirts, crying and whimpering, "Ghost, Mummee, Ghost, Mummee!" But his mother did not believe in ghosts, and she loosened his grasp and hid him behind a boulder, bidding him to stay there quietly until she came back. She walked toward the figure, which seemed to move away as she approached, and it was not until she could almost touch it that she discovered it to be an old white cow! Evidently, it had wandered down from one of the upper pastures, perhaps for a drink from the brook.

"Oh!" exclaimed Aunt Nellie, with a shudder, "Wasn't she plucky! I never could have done it! I'd have run all the way back – somewhere!"

"I don't believe I could have, either," replied Aunt Ella, and went on to finish her story. It seems that Mrs. Hazeltine did not live a great while, and the Little's took Jimmie into their home and Walker was appointed his guardian. The old place had been left alone to fall into decay as it was now, but Jimmie had found a good home and kindly people. He had grown to manhood there and was a great help and comfort to the aging couple.

Just as she completed the talk, the children joined them, clamoring for luncheon, "Cause they were just 'bout starved," they declared. So the things were spread out on a red and white table cloth, and Bert said, "Now we can pitch in and eat," and they certainly did! There were biscuits split and buttered and spread with chopped ham and pickles, white and dark sandwiches of chicken and cottage cheese, hard boiled eggs, cookies and doughnuts, tiny cucumbers peeled and rolled in vinegar and salt, apples, peaches, plums – oh what a feast – and oh how they *ate*!

And then to top it all, from the box she had carried so carefully, Aunt Ella produced a big chocolate pie, - and I *mean* a big one! Yum-Yum! So big, it was cut into seven big, good sized wedges, one for everyone present!

And when, at last, everyone was filled to capacity, and not even Frank or Bert could take another bite, they all declared it had been the best lunch ever! They cleared things away, scattering the crumbs so the birds could have a feast too, and Aunt Ella put the food that was left back in boxes, "just in case anyone gets hungry before we start for home!"

Then they discovered that Jennie had fallen fast asleep with her curly head in an empty plate! So they made her comfortable with a shawl for a pillow and Bert's blouse for a blanket, and everyone relaxed to recover from the effects of the feast just finished.

But sitting still soon proved irksome to Millie, who began coaxing her mother to tell them a story. Aunt Ella spoke up and said, "I've been thinking it would be fun if we played we were at an entertainment, and everybody taking a turn doing something to amuse the rest." Her listeners looked rather dubious, but she went right on. "Of course we'd have to plan the program a little before we started. I think Aunt Nellie will read you a story, for I saw her slip one of Millie's books in her bag," and Aunt Nellie nodded her assent. "Frank," the self-appointed manager went on, "You're the oldest of the children, so suppose we take you first. Now then, what will you do to help?"

Frank was a little shy with grown-ups, and blushed and stammered as he replied, "Aw Miz' Paige, I can't do nuthin'! I'd rather listen to the rest. I dunno how to entertain folks!"

"Fib!" she replied, shaking a finger at him. "You can certainly play a tune on your mouth organ, if you have it with you. I've heard you play and I think you do it wonderfully!"

"Oh, *that*?" returned Frank, disparagingly, "Sure, I can do *that* if you want me to. It's in my blouse pocket – I always have it with me." And he ran over to his blouse and got it cheerfully.

"Now, who's next? Millie, I guess." Millie had been so made of by the boarders at her home in Boston, and was so used to amusing them that she was anything but shy. So she replied off-handedly. "All right I'll speak a piece I learned for last day of school."

"Josie?" said her mother, smiling at Millie's self-possession, seeing that Josie was speechless with embarrassment, she went on, helpfully, "Josie writes little stories and poems sometimes, and I think she does them very well. Couldn't you repeat one for us dear?"

We-ell," Josie stammered as everyone clapped encouragingly, "I wrote one just this morning before breakfast. It isn't very good, but I'll read it to you – if I've got to do anything." And was rewarded by a smile from her mother and "that's my good girl!"

Then suddenly she called out, "Hey there, young man! Where are you going?" For she had spied Bert just in time, as he was silently trying to slip away! Looking crestfallen at being caught, he came back, muttering, "Aw Mama! You *know* I can't do nuthin'. I can't speak pieces or play a mouth organ,. I don't wanta be in the ole entertainment anyway!"

"But that wouldn't be fair, Bert. Everyone should help you know."

"Well then – what are *you* goin' to do?" he asked, turning the tables on her. At her look of consternation, everybody laughed so uproariously that Jennie woke up and came toddling over to see what was going on. When they quieted down a little Bert went back to the attack. "Well? What *are* you going to do, Mama?"

After a second's hesitation, she answered, "Er - - well, I don't really know myself, just yet, but I'll do something – and that's a promise."

Bert was congratulating himself on his escape, thinking the matter was closed, but Frank shattered the illusion by asking, "Miz' Page, does it count if two people do something together?"

"I don't see why that wouldn't be all right. Why?"

"All right then," he replied. "Then I'll play my 'monica, and Bert can dance a jig. He can dance an awful good jig, "Miz' Paige."

"Why that will be just grand!" Exclaimed Bert's mother, much surprised, for she had been totally unaware of her son's talents as a dancer!

And so the matter was settled, and they all adjusted themselves comfortably to enjoy the impromptu entertainment, which I assure you was an immense success.

Frank and Bert brought down the house with the peppy rendition of "Turkey in The Straw," and a lively jig. An encore was demanded, but Bert refused to cut any more capers, so Frank obliged with "Juanita" and "I was Seeing Nellie Home."

Millie's recitation of "The Bad Little Girl in School" convulsed them all, even her mother who had, of course, heard it before. But it was quite a long selection, so she too refused an encore.

Then Josie rose, with scarlet cheeks, and fishing a crumpled piece of paper from her pocket, delivered the following poem, very seriously and with much expression, not leaving out her name at the close.

God made this pretty world,
And he made the grass and flowers.
He made the sun and everything that's nice, --
But I wish he hadn't made the thunder showers!
God made the pretty little birds
And fishes, and tadpoles in the lakes.
He made the cunning little squirrels-
But I wish he hadn't made the snakes!
By Josephine Ella Paige.

There was a gale of laughter, and riotous clapping, enough to warrant *three* encores, but overcome with her success as a poetess, she dove down and hid her face in her mother's lap.

After they had somewhat recovered from the effects of this literary offering, Bert piped up, "And now it's Mama's turn! What are you going to do?" Everyone looked at her with curiosity and interest, for she had never been one to exhibit any special talent, and they all wondered what she would offer in the line of entertainment.

"Well," she replied, with twinkling eyes, and one of her mysterious smiles, "I think I'll introduce you to the "Who's This" family, - and let you do some guessing." She got up and started across the field toward the house, arms swinging, head bent forward and knees bent, with such long swinging steps they were almost a lope. There was a loud burst of laughter, and shouts of "That's Papa! That's Uncle David!" and "Mr. Paige, Mr. Paige!"

Bowing gracefully at their appreciation, she came back toward them at her natural walk, saying "and who is this?" The reply was unanimous. "That's you, that's you! And she bowed again "You're very good guessers," she said, "So maybe you can tell who this is," and she puffed out her cheeks, drew down her mouth, stuck out her lower lip and whined, "I don't see why I have to do dishes all the time!" Everyone laughed and looked at Josie, who hung her head and started to pout. But when her mother pouted right back, her sense of humor came to the rescue and she joined in the general laughter.

Everyone was surprised at Aunt Ella's gift of mimicry, as she imitated neighbors and friends, always in a kindly way, however. When she finally finished and sat down, they all relaxed again and sat talking over the entertainment and declaring it had been fun. And suddenly Jennie surprised them by thrusting out her underlip, and saying aggrievedly, "Jennie say sunfin', too!" Whereupon her mother hugged her and stood her on her feet, saying "Why of course Jennie can say something too. Go ahead, darling."

Jennie beamed upon them impartially, smoothed down her dress, and repeated gravely: "Suffer lil chillen come unto me, and bid them not."

No one clapped or laughed at Jennie's contribution to the entertainment, but she got hugged all round, and was perfectly satisfied with that appreciation.

The four older children took one more dip in the brook, while the mothers began packing away the things. Jennie was again seated in the express wagon, and they began the long, uphill trek homeward. They were quieter than on the walk down, for they were tired, although everyone was happy.

No one was very hungry, either, so they had crackers and milk and berries for supper, and were very early going to bed.

The children were asleep as soon as their heads touched the pillows, but for some time Aunt Nellie lay smiling in the dark as she recalled Josie's "But I wish he hadn't made the snakes!" And downstairs, Aunt Ella lay smiling too, with a heart full of love and tenderness, thinking of baby Jennie and her Bible verse.

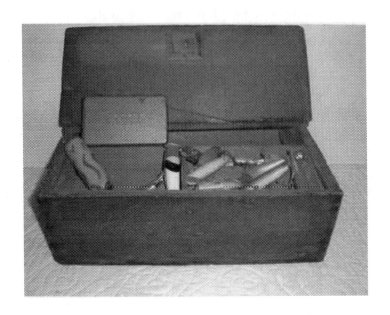

Chapter VI

The Saturday following the picnic at Harry Brook, Millie's father was to arrive for a two week's vacation, and she was so excited at the thought of seeing him again she could hardly contain herself. Josie and Bert were in almost the same state, for they were anxious to see if he could possibly be as wonderful as Millie declared him to be – quite the most wonderful man in the world! Privately, however, they didn't believe he would prove to be one bit superior to their own daddy!

Millie had been permitted to go with Joe to meet the train and her two chums seated themselves in the hammock the moment they saw the train crossing the Intervale, but it seemed a very long time after that before old Samson came into sight round the curve at the Schoolhouse. And when he did, a sudden streak of bashfulness attacked them both, so that instead of running down to meet them as had been planned, both dashed for the house and stood with their mother and Aunt Nellie on the door rock!

But at last they arrived and Joe drove into the yard, and then the great and wonderful man hopped out and lifted his small daughter to the ground. It was a little too soon for Bert and Josie to feel quite sure of his status, but he looked very pleasant and friendly, and he certainly was "comical," for he grabbed Aunt Nellie right off the rock in spite of her squeals, swinging her round in the air as if she weighed no more than Millie, winding up with a resounding kiss! After he had put her back on the door rock, safe and sound, he shook hands cordially with Aunt Ella, and turned to the children, who stood hand in hand, watching him with fascinated eyes.

"Well, well, well!" he exclaimed, "This must be Josie and Bert," shaking hands with them both. "And where is Jennie?" He went on "Seems to me I've heard there was a Jennie, too."

Aunt Ella laughed and said, "Oh yes, there's a Jennie all right, only she's having a nap. She'll be hopping out any minute now."

Millie, who had been clinging to his coat tails all this time, evidently could wait no longer, for shaking them vigorously, she cried. "Papa, did you bring me a present?"

He opened his mouth and his eyes wide, and pretended to be much astonished at the question. "Present!" He exclaimed, "Present? Was I supposed to bring you a present? Now if you can tell me one single reason why I should do such a silly thing as that, I'd like to hear it!"

Millie didn't seem much alarmed, but went on shaking his coat, much as a young puppy will worry a rag, and replied, "Cause I'm the onliest little girl you've got so 'course you ought to bring me a present! What *did* you bring me, Papa?"

So, seeing no way out of his dilemma, he laughed and said, "You'll have to wait till after dinner, young woman. I can't be playing Santa Claus till after I've had my dinner!"

"Of course you can't!" exclaimed Aunt Ella, "And you must be just about starved! Josie dear, run and get a pitcher of cold water from the well, please, - and I'll go and get dinner right on the table."

While she was doing so, Jennie came toddling out, and upon seeing a stranger, at once climbed into her high chair, from which vantage point she eyes him warily. Evidently she decided he was acceptable, for suddenly she bestowed a beautiful smile on him, and when he blinked his eyes at her rapidly, she laughed and blinked right back.

As usual, there was a bountiful dinner, - slices of pink, home cured ham in crisp fried slices, surrounded by gold and white fried eggs, new potatoes, cucumbers and tomatoes, spiced watermelon rind, and a great platter of hot, golden sweet corn. And to top off the feast, an Indian Pudding, with plenty of thick cream. And did they eat! They certainly did, with Millie and Bert racing as usual to see which would eat the most corn. But they had to yield the palm to the new comer, for he beat them by several ears.

However, although he appeared to be paying strict attention to his dinner, he had not failed to notice the change in his wife and daughter. The city pallor was gone and both were brown as hazelnuts, Millie freckled as a tiger lily into the bargain. He felt a wave of gratitude toward Aunt Ella, to whom he rightfully gave the credit.

The pudding and last swallow of coffee disappeared and seeing that the children were fidgeting restlessly, their elders took pity on them and adjourned to the sitting room. Uncle Lyman, (we might as well begin calling him so now as later) brought in one of the big bags that Joe had deposited in the front hall, and pretended to be having a dreadful time with straps and locks. But he gave it up when Millie sputtered to Josie, "He's doin' that just on purpose, Josie! He's a turrible tease! He could open that bag just as easy!" And sure enough, in half a minute the straps were loose and back went the cover. There was a deep sigh of relief from the children

He reached in and brought out a package, saying, to everyone's surprise, "Why, this doesn't seem to be for Millie! That's queer, but this says 'Master Bert Paige!' Now how on earth do you suppose that got into my bag?" And he handed the parcel to Bert who took it as if he thought it might contain dynamite.

But even this didn't seem to alarm his daughter much, for she shook her head at Josie, as if to say again, "He's a turrible tease!"

Again he reached into the bag and said, "And I'll be blest if this one doesn't say 'Miss Josephine Paige.' Here you are Josie," The little girl stepped forward and took the gift, smiling shyly, but saying very politely, "Oh, thank you Mr. Rumney," Whereupon Bert came back to earth and made them all laugh by saying, "Me too, - Thank you."

"Well, I declare, if here isn't something for the 'onliest little girl I've got! Right this way, Miss Rumney," which was a wholly wasted order, for she was already right there, one arm clutched round his neck, the other hugging her package.

"Now, seems to me there ought to be something here for a little girl named Jennie," he said, poking round in the bag as if in search of something. Jennie immediately slid down from her mother's lap and trotted over, to peer intently into the bag, and saying engagingly, "Sumfin' for Jennie? Me Jennie, me Jennie," sending them all into gales of laughter. Uncle Lyman took out a package, and said, "Yes, but don't I get anything for this?" She reached for the parcel, looked at him gravely a moment, and then said, "Jennie give new man nice big kiss," and hastily depositing one on his cheek, darted back to her mother's lap.

Turning back to the bag, he brought forth a small package and read "Mrs. Ella Paige," and handed it to Millie to deliver, for Aunt Ella's lap was full of Jennie and her bundle. She was so surprised that she could only stammer her thanks but her cheeks were pink with surprise and pleasure.

"Er – is my wife present?" The 'turrible tease' inquired, making them all laugh by holding out a parcel and looking all about, pretending not to see her. "She certainly *is*, simpleton," Aunt Nellie exclaimed, and tried to box his ears when he handed out the last gift.

"Now," said Millie, dancing about with excitement, "Now let's open our presents," and there was a great snapping of string and rustling of paper, and such a chorus of "oh mys!" and "oh Me's" you couldn't have heard yourself think!

Bert found a wooden box, with hasp and padlock, and inside were tin trays and compartments filled with all sorts of things for fishing, - lines, hooks, sinkers, even "flies" which he had never seen before. Everything you could think of for fishing. Bert stared at it, wide eyes and speechless – poking about in the compartments in delight. Uncle Lyman hadn't forgotten Millie's first letter which told of Bert's penchant for fishing, and about his buying fish hooks with his precious "egg money!"

Uncle Lyman saw the boy's rapture altho' he hadn't made a sound, so he said offhandedly, "Any horn pout round here, Bert? Best eatin' I know of," and Bert came out of his trance in a second. "Lots of 'em in the upper brook, and down in Cy Hammond's pond too." He replied. And when Uncle Lyman said "fine! How about you and I goin' fishin' some night next week?" he then and there made a life-long friend of Bert.

Josie's packet held a box too, but one made of delicious smelling sweet grass, lined throughout with pale blue satin, and equipped with needle book, needles, pins, a thimble, scissors, and all colors of thread and silk! "Oh look, Mama! Look Millie!" She gasped. "Isn't it lovely? Look Mama! Now I won't have to be asking you for things to sew with!" And clasping her workbox closely, she turned and thanked Uncle Lyman again.

"Yes it's awful pretty, Josie," Millie said, admiringly. "I guess he 'membered what I wrote him bout how nice you sewed, little teensy, weenie stitches!"

Then she proudly showed her gift, a pretty little maple lap desk, filled with paper and envelopes, pencils, pen, ruler, and ten two cent stamps.

"I chose that for my 'onliest' girl, because she writes me such nice letters," said her father, smiling at her evident delight in the little desk.

"I'll write lots better ones now. Not this summer, 'cause you're right here now, - but I will next summer, Papa, when I come back here."

Uncle Lyman and the two mamas exchanged looks and smiles, but he said, apparently quite seriously "Oh! Then you're expecting to come back next summer? Supposing your Aunt Ella has decided she's had about all the Tom Boys she wants?"

Millie looked horrified, and turned to Aunt Ella with such a stricken face, that that lady laughed outright, and hastened to reassure her. "Don't you worry a mite about it, dear. I like boys and Tom Boys. You just come back the minute school is done. Why, what would Josie do now, if you didn't come back, or Bert, or any of us? And Josie stood smiling and nodding like a Chinese Mandarin.

Uncle Lyman had brought beautiful lace fichus to the two ladies, these being the "last word" in style at that time. Both were delighted, and had them draped about their shoulders already. Aunt Ella was having visions of "cutting a dash" when she appeared at Grange or Church in the lovely scarf.

And Jennie? She was lying back on her mother's lap hugging her gift tightly a lovely, wooly dog or was it a lamb? Evidently she had decided it was a lamb, for she was happily crooning over and over, "Baa, baa, B'ack sheep, Baa, baa B'ack Sheep," for all it's fleece was *white*, white as snow! It was soft and warm and cuddly, and for months she would not go to sleep unless her "B'ack sheep" was nestled close beside her.

But of course, all the excitement died down. The children wanted to show Uncle Lyman their play places and Aunt Nellie offering to help with the dishes, Josie was excused from her usual "chore," – and off they went.

He was escorted through the barn and carriage house, where he agreed that the surrey was a handsome one and led to Big Rock, where he actually had the temerity to poke a stick down the snake hole! And they went over to the brook, and to the back pasture to see Pegasus and the cows. They had a wonderful time, but Uncle Lyman was not sorry to get back to the house, and drop into the hammock.

It was a Saturday, so Uncle David arrived as usual, on the afternoon train. After supper they all sat down under the Maples; Millie perched on her father's knee and Josie on her father's. (Jennie being abed and asleep with her b'ack sheep.) The two men got to 'reminiscencing" about the Civil War, while the rest listened spell bound. They found that although they had served under different States, they had fought in several of the same battles. But bed time arrived for the children, who were nodding sleepily, tired after a long, but happy day, so after making many tentative plans for good times to come, they trotted docilely off to bed. And the elders soon followed, and Paige Hill Farm settled down to a quiet, peaceful night.

Next day, sure enough, the good times began and continued straight through the last two weeks of the stay in Goffstown.

There were drives in the surrey, Uncle Lyman as Driver-in-Chief, with three able assistants, sometimes four, when Frank went along, too. Once or twice, however, Joe's buggy was borrowed and Uncle Lyman and Aunt Nellie would slip away from the rest for a drive by themselves.

One day was spent down at the river, and, of course, one at Harry Brook, at the children's special request, for Uncle Lyman *must* see Harry Brook.

And one day, with several of the neighbors, they drove up to the top of Uncanoonuc for another picnic. They went in the big hayrack, with two horses, and Joe for the driver. Uncle Lyman and the children scoured the woods the day before, gathering ground pine, and hemlock boughs. That evening they made long ropes of the pine, and early next morning wove it all round the hay rack, and tied hemlock boughs to the uprights. It certainly looked gorgeous! The bottom was covered with straw and there were stools and boxes for those who did not wish to sit on the floor.

They sang and told stories all the way. Most of them walked up the mountain itself, for it was quite a pull, even for two horses. And such a dinner! Quite as good as the one at the famous picnic at Harry Brook, only this time the piece de resistance being, not a chocolate pie, but two huge watermelons, donated by Uncle Lyman. He showed them how the people down South could eat the melon and flip the seeds out of the side of their mouths, and gales of laughter flowed as everyone tried it!

And of course Bert and Frank and Uncle Lyman went fishing several times, so they had all the "messes" of horn pout they wanted.

There were walks and rides to the Village, with treats of ice cream or candy, often both, ice cream in plates, *never once* in scoops! And not paid for with eggs, either!

But inexorably the days fled by, and the frost of September came. On the next Monday there had to be a parting, much to everyone's sorrow, for the Boston Schools opened on Wednesday, and the little Red School House a few days later.

And so summer ended, and the day of departure arrived. There were copious tears from Josie and Millie, until Jennie, in an excess of sympathy, puckered her lips and howled lustily, whereat tears turned to laughter. The two girls swore eternal friendship, and agreed to write to one another. They did, too, childish letters, of course, but starting a correspondence that never ceased. There were promises of a return the next summer. "Just the minute I get out of school," Millie said. And at last there was the final drive behind old Samson, to the Village, - the little train was boarded – and the trip to Boston was begun.

Again a little girl stood with nose against the window as the train puffed through the covered bridge, across the river, and whistled at the Fair Ground crossing. But suddenly, as it started across the Intervale, the passengers were startled and amused as the child cried loudly. "Look Papa! Look Mama! There's Paige Hill, and there's Aunt Ella's house! I bet Josie and Bert are waving at me – they said they would!" and she frantically waved a diminutive handkerchief.

She could almost SEE her summer chums, so sure was she that they were out on the lawn waving. And they were there, waving Aunt Ella's big white worsted shawl, all the while the train was crossing the long Intervale. Waved until with a final, faint whistle, it passed out of sight, beyond Yacum Hill.

Chapter VII

The winter went by in its usual manner on Paige Hill, full of busy days, - more "chores" to do, for more wood was needed with several stoves to keep going, and there were paths to be dug through the deep snows, and school to go to, and long cozy evenings. These they all loved. Aunt Ella was usually busy with sewing or mending, but could nearly always take part in guessing games or puzzles. Sometimes they made and pulled candy, or there was corn to pop, or apples to be brought up from the cellar, or butternuts from the attic to be shelled and picked out, or Christmas presents for Josie and Aunt Ella to be making.

Often some of the neighbors dropped in, or perhaps they went calling, and always books to read. Oh, there was plenty to do, and lots of fun to be had during the long winter months.

And life in Boston was going on about as usual too. Of course there were no wood boxes to be filled, or dishes to be done, or candy making, for until she was thirteen, they boarded in the big house on Temple Street. There were long evenings there too, perhaps not such merry ones as in Goffstown, for there was only one little girl. Sometimes she stayed in her grandma's room, which she loved to do, for grandma was a tireless reader, and Millie loved being read to. Or sometimes she would call on some of the other boarders, or go to the theater, which perhaps she loved best of all, for the love of theatricals was born in her. She often amused the boarders re-enacting the whole play, next day, but oftenest she entertained them by relating some of her experiences in Goffstown.

And of course there was school, and coasting, and playing with her friends. But still, all winter, while the Paige children were saying "When Millie comes," she was saying, "When I go back to Goffstown," so the longing for a reunion was mutual.

Christmas came with its presents and decorations and trees, a box from Boston and one to Boston, the one with a brooch for Aunt Ella, a dress length for Josie, a book for Bert and a dolly that said "Mama" for Jennie. The other held beautiful shiny red Mackintosh apples, polished to a fare-you-well by Josie's strenuous rubbing, a box each of chestnuts, shagbarks and butternuts, a jar of cookies, a box of molasses candy

– all packed round with spicy hemlock, and sprays of ground pine and partridge berries! I don't know which box gave the most pleasure – but do not believe there was much choice.

And then, in March, came a BIG surprise, - a brand new baby! A new baby called Flora! And soon after that, real Spring arrived, and a lovely box of Arbutus went winging away to Boston! But at last, after what seemed endless waiting, school closed, and lo! There was Millie, perched high in Joe's wagon, driving old Samson in great style – and barefooted! Aunt Ella didn't draw back this time, but went forward and lifted her down from the wagon. She looked so surprised at seeing the bare feet that Aunt Nellie laughed and said, "My land, Ella, she had them off before we got to Parker's Store!"

And so the second summer began where the first left off. Of course, new things were discovered or invented, it is really funny what four small people, for Jennie was trotting round with them now, can find to do!

Millie declared the new baby was "perfectly darling" – for she certainly did love babies. It was well she did, too, for they seemed to appear quite often at Paige Farm, Flora this time and in due course, Florence and Bertha.

If we wrote of everything they did each separate summer, this book would be as long as the World History, so we will not attempt it, nor to keep their "doings" in chronological order. But we will try to tell of some of the events, happenings, pranks and escapades, hoping we will not weary our readers into giving up the book entirely.

Chapter VIII

One morning Josie and Millie woke to find rain coming down in torrents.
"Oh dear," wailed Millie, sitting up in bed. "Just look at it pouring! Now we can't do one single thing! I wish it would *never* rain!"

But Josie, always the optimist, answered cheerfully, "Why, no you don't Millie Rumney! You don't wish any such thing! We wouldn't have any water in the wells, nor any over at the brook, nor down at Harry Brook, or the river, - an' the grass an' flowers would all die!"

"Oh, I know that," responded Millie. "'Corse I don't exactly mean *never* rain. But seems to me if I'd been arrangin' the weather, I'd fix it so it would only rain nights! I don't see what we'll do all day, just the same."

"Pooh, we always find *something* to do, don't we?" returned Josie. "'Sides, it'll prob'ly clear off by and by. Mama always says, "Rain before seven, clear before 'leven," and she hopped out of bed cheerfully,.

"Well, I just hope she's right, that's all. I'll just 'bout bust if we have to stay in all day. What'll we do first?" She asked, and sank back to her pillow.

Josie considered the matter a moment, and then said, "I know what. Let's Spring clean our play house, up in the attic."

"You can't Spring clean in August, can you?" returned Millie, certainly a little contrary this morning.

"'Course you can, Ninny," was the reply. "Didn't we play exploring the Arctic the other day, an' nearly freeze? You can *play* anything, can't you? We can make b'lieve it's April, an' that we're way behind with the cleaning – an'go for the play house like anything!"

"Going like anything" always appealed to the young lady still sprawled out on the bed, and her vivid imagination was already at work. She bounced out of bed, and began scrabbling into her clothes, trying to catch up with Josie, who was combing her hair.

"We can make dust caps," she said, "'an' move the furniture all round. House work is awful hard work, though. Oh, I know – we can play Jennie an' Flora work out, an' hire them to help. Hey! Wait for me!" She cried, as she saw Josie, completely attired, opening the door.

"You haven't brushed your teeth," said that young lady, sternly.

"I know it, but I've got to brush 'em after breakfast anyhow," the delinquent replied. "Mama makes me do it ef'ry time I eat, an' I did brush 'em after supper – an' haven't eaten since."

"You have too," contradicted Josie. "Didn't we bring up dried apples an' crackers, an' eat 'em in bed last night?"

"Well, I don't care, I won't stop now – I'll brush 'em extra good after breakfast. I'm just about starved right this minute. Oh, come on, - let's get down stairs to breakfast!" And off they dashed, clattering noisily down the stairs.

They found the rest of the family half through breakfast, and after hurried "good morning," they started in on their cereal as if they really *were* half starved. All through the meal they aired their plans about Spring cleaning, until Jennie and Flora became enthused, - which had been exactly what they intended. Even Aunt Ella must have approved of the idea, for she told them they would find plenty of dusters and cleaning rags in the rag bag, just inside the shed. "I would suggest, however," she said, "that you sweep and dust the whole attic rather than just your play part, and wipe off the trunks and boxes. And you might brush some of the cob webs off the window, while you are in the cleaning business."

For a moment, there was a hush, for this began to look like *real* work, more than a game! But presently Josie said, "We will Mama. Wouldn't be much sense in cleaning just our play houses – and let your part go dirty! Maybe we'll even wash the window!"

Her mother let the reference to "your part" go without comment, although she could have replied and justly, that the clutter all over the place was certainly none of *her* making. But she forbore and let the matter rest.

The dishes were soon done and the beds made, and up they trooped, laden with broom, cleaning cloths, soap, basin and a pail of warm water. April or August, Spring or Summer, that attic certainly got a cleaning! They tugged all the trunks and boxes out from under the eaves, swept thoroughly, and moved them back again. Then they swept the rest of the floor and put all the rubbish in an old carton for disposal later.

"My goodness!" Josie exclaimed, puffing after such exertion, "I never saw such a mess – an' I guess we must have made it, 'cause I helped Mama clean it this Spring – an' nobody comes up here much but us!"

"Prob'ly we don't pick up after ourselves," said Millie, Quite undisturbed by this statement. "Mama says *I* never do, an' grandma said I never would till she stopped doin' it for me."

They dusted after the dust had had time to settle, and Jennie washed the window, which had sadly needed it. It was surprising how much lighter the attic seemed to be after the removal of cobwebs, fly specks, dead wasps and just plain dirt.!

When this was done they sank down with sighs of weariness and relief, and at that very moment, Aunt Ella's head appeared at the head of the stairs. She was carrying a tray, and the four girls gave four whoops of delight, for on it was a pitcher of cold milk, five cups, for Florence was with her, and a plate of sugar cookies!

"I thought you ladies might be hungry after such a strenuous morning," she said, looking round the room with wide eyes. "My, my! But you certainly have done a good job! And to cheer you up, although you seem to be cheerful enough, - it is going to clear off. The sky is quite light over in the West."

After she had gone back down stairs, the "ladies" set the little table in the play house, and sat munching cookies and sipping milk, until they were completely recovered from their exhausting exertions.

Suddenly, just as they were finishing their lunch, Millie, who had apparently been admiring the results of the morning's labors, asked, "Josie, where does that hole go to?" And pointed to an opening under the eaves.

"I don't know," Josie returned, "But I guess it must go out over the shed. The Buttery must be right under there."

"What you s'pose is in there?"

"Nuthin' much, I guess. It's so dark in there, nobody'd put anything there, 'sides there's room enough in the attic for lots more things without pokin' into that dark hole!"

"Let's go look anyhow," Millie went on curiously, and started toward the opening.

Jennie gave a little squeal and cried, "Mercy sakes, Millie, don't go in there! I peeked in once, but it's awful dark – there's no window, just a little hole at the other end of it. There's nothin' in there anyhow."

"How do you know there isn't? Did you go in?"

"My goodness, no. I guess I didn't!"

"Then how do you know there isn't anything there?" the persistent inquirer continued, relentlessly.

Jennie was silenced, but Josie said, impatiently, "Well, lan' sakes, Millie, if you want to know what's in there so bad, why don't you go look for yourself?" and then was surprised at Millie's emphatic, "I'm goin' to!"

"O-oh!" exclaimed Jennie, "I should think you'd be scared to death! It's an awful spooky lookin' place!"

At the word "spooky" Flora immediately started for the stairs, grabbing Florence by the hand, and stammering, "I g-guess I'll g-go down s-stairs!" The idea of exploring "spooky" places didn't appeal to her in the least. But curiosity won, and she seated herself on the top step from which there was a speedy exit in case any spooks appeared.

Josie and Jennie were by this time as curious as their questioner who had gone over to the hole, and Josie, who never deserted her chum, exclaimed, "Oh, all right! If you're bound to look, I will too!"

So side by side, they dropped to their knees and peered through the opening, with Jennie standing close behind them. At first it did appear pitchy black inside, but as soon as their eyes became accustomed to it, they saw that a dim light came through the smaller opening, and that it was from the shed.

"I wouldn't go in, Millie," said Josie as she felt her companion edge forward a little. "Maybe there's no flooring in there!"

"There's boards – I can see 'em," was the reply. "I'll feel ahead with my hands," and she crept in inch by inch, her faithful follower close behind. Once inside there was more light, which came from the attic rather than from the shed. It was low, just high enough for them to stand, stooping a little, and as Josie had said, it was evidently directly over the Buttery.

At first, they thought there was nothing whatever in the small space, but just as they were about to go back, Josie exclaimed, "There's something, Millie! It's a box or something. See? Over there in the corner."

They crawled over, but could not make out what it was. They tried to pull it forward away from the eaves, but it was bulky and heavy, and they could only move it a little. And just then they heard Bert's voice.

"Who's up there?" he demanded. "What you doin' up there?" He had heard their voices as he came through the side door into the shed, but could not locate them exactly. "Who's up there?" he repeated.

"Us." Came the muffled reply. "Oh Bert, come on up – we've found somethin'."

"Up *where*? Where in tunket are you, anyway?" By this time he was pretty sure where they were, but couldn't imagine how they got there.

"Come up to the attic." They instructed, "Hurry!" and he scampered through the Buttery and up the attic stairs and was soon crawling in after the girls. With this reinforcement, Flora and Florence joined Jennie, and waited with interest to see what was to come.

"What on earth you in *here* for?" was Bert's opening remark. Of course he had seen the opening before, but it had never occurred to him to investigate.

"Just wanted to know what was in here," replied Millie, calmly. "That's all there is, though," and she pointed to the box or whatever it was.

"What is it?" he asked.

"We don't know," answered Josie, "But it's awful clumsy."

Bert took hold and tugged, moving it a little, and then exclaimed, "Why it's upside down! That's what makes it so heavy. Come on, you take hold too, an' we can turn it over."

With their joint efforts, they turned it over and then Bert proposed getting it out into the attic where they could see what it was. So he and Josie pulled and Millie pushed till they got it through the hole into the light.

They stood and stared at it, no wiser than before as to what it was. It was not a box, although somewhat like one – a queer looking contraption at any rate. The four sides slanted outward so that the top was somewhat larger than the bottom. It was made of heavy wood, nearly an inch thick unpainted or varnished, but smoothed to a satiny finish. They studied it intently.

"I bet you it's a baby's cradle," opened Millie.

"Cradle!" exclaimed Josie, "A cradle has rockers, an' this hasn't any rockers!"

"Maybe it's just a bed, - a baby's bed," suggested Jennie, and Josie assented.

"I guess that's what it is," she said, but Bert was still studying it.

"Golly!" he finally cried, "Maybe it was a baby's bed. I wouldn't be s'prised, but you know what? It'd make a *dandy* boat! We could take it over to the brook an' float all round the pond! I could even make the dam a little higher so's the pond would be bigger, an' I can make a paddle. We could have a lot of fun!"

Florence threw her vote in favor of said plan at once, by clambering over the side and sitting down, saying "Boat – nice boat. Fl'ence goin' for ride."

They all laughed, and there was a general murmur of enthusiasm, till Josie put a spoke in it with "We'll have to ask Mama. Maybe it's something we can't have," And at that possibility, there was a stampede for the stairs, all but Florence, who placidly continued her ride. They clattered down yelling "Mama! Aunt Ella! Mama!" scaring that lady half out of her wits, thinking something must have happened.

They all clamored at once, clutching, pulling and pushing her toward the attic stairs and up, where they pointed to the "boat," with its passenger. She looked at it wonderingly, and asked, "What is it! Where did you get it? I never saw it before."

They showed her the opening under the eaves, and explained all talking at once, while Florence was peacefully murmuring, "De tap, ole boat, de tap!" a little mixed in her metaphors.

After the explanations, plans and coaxing for permission to take it over to the brook died down a little, Aunt Ella contrived to get a word in edgewise, "Yes," she said, "I can see that it looks like a boat, but supposing it leaks and you get drowned?"

"Get *drowned*?" they hooted scornfully. "Drowned – over in the brook?" and Bert went on, "Why Mama, 'taint a foot deep anywhere's! Can't we have it, *please*, Mama?"

She settled the matter temporarily, by replying, "Listen children, I never saw this-er-boat before and have no idea what it really is. So far as I am concerned you may have it and welcome, but it must have belonged to Grandma Paige, or Grandpa. So you will have to wait and ask Papa about it Saturday."

"Saturday!" Josie wailed, "Not till then?" and her mother laughed and replied, "Silly! That's only day after tomorrow, and we go to the Village tomorrow, of course, so you couldn't do much about it anyway."

So they brightened up, and as she went down the stairs, she heard Bert say, "Well, you girls better be cleanin' the dust off of it. I'm goin' right straight out to the carriage house an' get a board I got hid out there, an' make a paddle. I'm goin' to be on the safe side an' have it ready, 'cause I bet Papa'll let us have it." And off he flew to be "on the safe side."

Sure enough, he was right about his father, for dragged up to inspect the find almost on the instant of his arrival, the entire family in tow; he looked at it and laughed heartily.

"Where on earth did you find that?" he exclaimed. "Why I haven't laid eyes on that since I was your age, Bert. That's mother's old bread trough!"

"Bread trough!" Aunt Ella repeated. "I never heard of one."

"Yes, Mother used to mix bread in it, probably eight or ten loaves at a time. Most people in the old days had them, especially if they had big families."

"Can we have it?" and then anxiously, "Mama, do you want it to mix bread in?"

"Heaven forbid!" she replied soulfully, and she and Uncle David laughed together. "You may have it so far as I'm concerned."

"And as far as I'm concerned, too," Uncle David added. But he laughed again when he heard they wanted it for a *boat*.

"A boat? Hmmm, well, it will probably leak like a sieve. You'd better fill it with water and stones and sink it for a couple of days, while the wood swells. That ought to tighten it up. How were you expecting to get it down stairs and over to the brook? Pretty heavy, isn't it?"

Bert said he guessed it was, and had been worrying about that a little, but he breathed a sign of relief when he noticed the twinkle in his fathers' eye. "Well," he said, "I'll take it over to the barn for you after supper. And Bert, find a wide enough board for it to ride on, and hitch Pegasus to it when you take him to pasture in the morning. He can haul it to the brook for you.

So there they were in full possession of a *boat* – and all the difficulties of transportation settled. It was really wonderful how easily Papa solved almost insurmountable problems!

The boat *did* leak, a lot at first, and a little always, but it floated, - and after all, what difference does it make, sitting in a little water, more or less?

They paddled; taking turns of course, for only one could ride at a time, up and down and around the pond. Bert and Millie, always more adventurous than the rest, even paddled up the brook as far as they could, playing they were explorers, trying to find the source of the Amazon. But it was gloomy, the shallow water dirty and muddy, and "snakey" and they were constantly running aground, so they soon discarded that, and contented themselves in the bright, sunny pool instead.

Oh, it was fun, I can tell you. I often wonder what Grandma Paige would have thought if she had seen her bread trough transformed into a *boat*! But if she had, and known the hours and hours of fun and pleasure her grand-children and their little friends had with it, I am quite sure she would have laughed and said, "Well, bless their little hearts!"

Dough Trough

Chapter IX

Josie and Millie were playing house out on Big Rock one morning in August, and had been bemoaning the fact that in a little more than three weeks, Millie would be going back to Boston. Even the fact that her father and mother would be up the next Saturday, did not cheer them up, as that would mean – only *two* weeks more together!

Bert came running round the corner of the house and started to join them but stopped at the edge of the lawn and stood gazing down the road.

"What you see, Bert?" called Millie, and Josie added, "Who's comin'?"

"Golly," he replied, "there's a whopping big load of lumber comin' up the road. No, there's *two of 'em!*" The girls ran over and stood watching with him. "Prob'ly goin' to Walker's," he said.

"Wonder what he's goin' to build with all that wood?" said Millie, and Bert gave her one of his superior looks and said, "Wood? That ain't wood, - that's lumber."

"Oh?" she returned, slightly annoyed at his tone. "An' what's lumber if it isn't wood, ---stone?"

"What is the difference, Bert?" asked Josie but before he could give them any further instruction, she went on, "Look, they didn't stop at Little's, they're comin' right up the hill."

"Prob'ly goin' up to Dunbarton or somewhere. Somebody buildin' a house most likely."

But just then the wagons had reached the top of the hill, and the horses stood with heaving sides, getting their breath after the long climb. And then, to the watchers' surprise, the two men on each team jumped down, and began unloading, putting the lumber from one team on the lawn close to the stone wall, and that from the other just across the road, under The Balm of Gilead tree.

Bert sauntered over, and after greeting the men, said, "Guess you've got the wrong place, haven't you?"

"That so?" Answered one of the drivers, with a grin. "Not unless Dave Paige has moved. Still livin' here, ain't he?" And he grinned again at the surprised look on the boys face.

The girls still stood watching, but Bert turned and streaked it for the house. "Mama!" he called, once inside and she answered from the pantry. "Mama, there's two big loads of lumber come, an' the men are unloadin' it. Is it ours Mama?"

"I guess it is," she replied, calmly. "I've been looking for it all week."

Bert's eyes popped open in surprise. "What's it for Mama? What we goin' to build, a new house?"

"Not this time," she replied, laughing. "The house can stand for some time yet, but the barn is getting pretty rickety. The underpinning has rotted away, and Papa says it won't be safe long, so we're going to have a nice, new one."

"A big one?"

His mother laughed and replied, "From what your father says I guess it will be *plenty* big! And it's going to have a cupola, think of that!"

"One you can go into – or just a make b'lieve one?"

"Oh it's to be a real one – with windows on all four sides."

Without another word, Bert dashed off to impart the wonderful news, and as Jennie and Flora had joined the others, he had quite an audience.

As soon as the wagons had unloaded and started back for the Village, the children began clambering over the two piles of lumber, and all the rest of the day, as more loads kept coming, they forsook their usual games in the enjoyment of this new pastime.

Window frames and sash and doors were stored in the carriage house till there was scarcely room to get in and out. And in a few days men came to tear down the old barn. Then more men came to haul in and lay a foundation, the great flat rocks that had been left in the barn yard some time before.

They built a temporary shed of some of the old lumber for Pegasus and the cows, and although Jennie sputtered that they would be lonesome for their old home, they did not appear to mind the change at all.

The three older children had watched the old barn being demolished with mixed emotions. Excitement and interest, of course, but with a vague sense of nostalgia for the dark, dusty old hay lofts, the stolen hens' nest, the jumps from the beams into the sweet smelling hay, the trapeze –oh they had wonderful times in the old barn, so that a little unhappiness was mixed with the excitement. But the prospects of a bigger barn and with a cupola too, soon offset the memories of the old one.

There was so much to see and do! Bert and Frank had begged for some of the old lumber, and were as busy as bees, building a real camp, big enough for them all to camp in, over in the pines beyond the brook. Millie's parents had arrived on schedule, and her Father was an immense help on the camp project, doing much of the roof, and the high nailing. He even showed them how to thatch the roof with old straw and hay, so that it was practically weather proof.

Millie hated to go back to Boston more than ever for she wanted to see the barn itself go up, but that was impossible, for Uncle David said it would not be up and ready for the first coat of paint before October. So she consoled herself by trying to imagine what it would look like from the train when she came back the following summer.

They had a grand time though, when the foundation rocks were laid and the enormous beams were placed on them for the underpinning, playing Circus. This time Millie posed as a wire walker, prancing forward and backward, standing on one foot, with the other gracefully (??) extended backward, and balancing a long pole in her hands! Poor Aunt Nellie nearly had nervous prostration for fear she would fall, - but she didn't. Bert had never seen a wire walker, but was greatly impressed with some of the things she described as their "stunts." He imitated all she did, and even tried pushing a wheelbarrow back and forth, as she declared real wire walkers did, only to have the wheelbarrow skid and take a dive off the beam! But he had sense enough to let go, or he would have gone with it!

The day before the exodus to Boston, they were all sitting out on the lawn after supper, when Millie suddenly said, "Aunt Ella, are you *sure* the barn will be done before I come back next summer?"

Aunt Ella laughed and said, "Well, I guess it had *better* be done. Poor Pegasus and my bossies wouldn't like spending the winter in the shed where they are now! And just think of my having to wade through snow way out there to milk!"

"Well, then," was the astonishing reply, "I can go home in peace. I'd hate to think I'd have to wait for a barn to play in! Now I can think how nice it's going to be – I can think 'bout it all winter."

"Yes dear, it is always pleasant to have something to look forward to," Aunt Ella replied.

Millie seemed to be studying the idea a few moments, and then remarked, -"Well, I've got an awful lot of nice things to look forward to, haven't I? There's the new barn, an' Big Rock, an' the new camp, an' the brook, an' Josie, an' the other kids, an' a new baby, prob'ly. There wasn't one this year, so I 'spect there'll be one next summer."

There was a shout of laughter from the grown-ups and for some reason Aunt Ella's cheeks were very, very pink. She looked over at Aunt Nellie and smiled, and then said, "Well, I guess you may safely look forward to one," and everybody laughed again.

Everyone but Josie. She was looking rather peculiar and studying her mother intently. After a moment she got up from her seat on the grass and said gravely, "Mama! IS there going to be another baby?"

Her mother blushed again, but replied quite as gravely, "Why yes, Josie, I think there is. Why, dear? I though you loved babies!" "I do love 'em," Josie answered, "But I think *five* of us is *plenty!* I've always wanted us to have a piano, but I guess we never will if this keeps up!" And she stalked across the lawn and into the house. The two women rocked with laughter, and Uncle Lyman rolled over and over on the grass in an ecstasy of mirth. Millie watched them wondering what was so funny, and then broke them all up again by stating emphatically, "Well, I think a piano would be awful nice too, but all the same, I'd rather have a baby *any* time!" and she ran after her chum to console her.

Chapter X

Millie was rather disappointed at her first view of the new barn, from the train the next June, for it appeared to be quite small, but it was vastly different when she came riding up the hill with Joe! It towered over the house, like a giant over a pigmy, tall and wide, and gleaming with white paint! And away up on top, the promised cupola perched, like a small hat on a very large head.

If she had had her way, she would have explored it at once, but dinner was ready and waiting and her mother well knew that the exploring would be a protracted affair, so she insisted upon dinner first. Besides, there was the new baby to see – and surely a new baby was more important than a new barn!

So the visit was postponed for awhile. The baby, Bertha, proved to be adorable, as dark as Flora and Florence were fair, with big dark eyes and black hair, like Bert's. Josie looked on while Millie admired, apparently having quite forgotten that she would have preferred a piano!

But at last dinner was eaten, Josie excused from dishes, as Millie's arrival warranted a celebration, so off they tore for the barn. The old one had been a dim and dusky place even on the brightest of days, there being no windows except the two small ones in the tie-up, and one up over the loft. But this was vastly different. There were two doors in front, the big sliding door, and an ordinary one at the side, and windows on the South side, and a door and two windows on the back. There was a built in silo – a weird looking and smelly place Millie thought when Bert opened the door and let her peer inside. The horse stall was back of it, and on the west side was the tie-up, much larger than the one in the old barn. And one didn't have to climb a ladder to the hay loft – there was a real stair case, two, in fact, for there were two lofts. The beams were much higher for jumping and she was anxious to try it, but there was too much to see to do so now.

But Bert was anxious to show her the cupola, so presently he led the way across the top loft and up a short flight of open stairs. She gasped with delight when she stepped into a little room perhaps eight feet square just room for them all without crowding. There was a large window on each side, and Bert took a pair of binoculars from a case hanging by one of them, and said grandly, "Here, take a look through *these,* an' I guess you'll be s'prised!" And she was, for Rattlesnake Ledge and even Manchester seemed almost as close as Gilmore's! From the back window, of course, there was nothing to be seen but the pines over beyond the brook, but from the one on the South, she could see the Village Road where it passed the Hammonds, and Lucians and Colbys, and here and there the river shining in the sun, and the Intervale beyond it, even the Mast Road, where teams looked like toy ones – and then the Mountains! Every tree and ledge and scattered farm house seemed within touching distance!

It was a wonderful place, that cupola. They stood discussing it for a few moments, and Bert saw that Millie was gazing out the East window with a sort of speculative look. He tried to fathom what was on her mind for he did not think it was the view, but could not seem to "get it." However, he found out a little later that right then and there an idea was 'hatching' – one that was to grow rapidly until it became a full fledged 'stunt.'

Later, when they had rejoined their mothers, Aunt Ella asked her what she thought of the new barn, and after a moment she replied. "Well, it's a *lovely* barn. I guess it's the nicest one in Goffstown – maybe in the whole world. It's awful big an' got an awful lot of nice places to play in – an' the cupola is just wonderful. I've got some wonderful plans, too. But I like the old barn too – an' you know – I'm kind of worryin' 'bout the hens! I don't b'lieve they can get way up to the hay now, it's so high up and how can they steal nests?"

After this lengthy discourse, there was silence for a moment, for Aunt Ella was turning over one remark – "I've got some wonderful plans too" – in her mind with some uneasiness! Sometimes Millie's plans were things to conjure with! But presently she replied, alluding to the last part of it only.

"No dear, I don't believe the hens could find a way up to the hay. In the first place, the door to the stairway is supposed to be kept closed, anyway. I don't want they *should* either. We've fenced in a big hen yard, and added to the hen house, so maybe they'll be contented to stay home and lay their eggs in the proper place!"

"But what will Josie and Bert do for egg money then!" Millie asked, anxiously.

Aunt Ella laughed and returned,, "Oh, so *that's* what's worrying you! Well, I have them collect *all* the eggs now, every day, and I pay them five cents a dozen. And they have decided they want to pick berries this year, too. A man comes round every Thursday and buys them."

"Yes," said Josie, "an' last Wednesday I got two boxes of early low ones over on the ledge, an' I got ten cents a box for them. They're pretty scarce now, but they'll be thick pretty soon. I'm goin' to pick every day an' earn a lot of money."

"Yes, but if you do that, when are we going' to *play*?" objected Millie.

Aunt Ella laughed again at seeing Millie's dejected face, and comforted her by saying "She won't need to pick every day, my dear. The berry man wants them fresh you know, for he ships them to Manchester and Boston. So it would be better just to pick Tuesdays and Wednesdays for him. Of course, we will have to pick a few for our own use. When the high bush blueberries come along, we could plan to all pick those two days and maybe take our dinners over to the pine woods for a sort of picnic."

Millie heaved a sigh of relief, and thought maybe she would pick too, and earn a lot of money." – at any rate, she knew there was to be plenty of time for play.

It seemed as if some new pleasure was always cropping up at Paige Farm, and this summer was no exception. One Saturday evening they were all sitting out on the lawn, when Uncle David proposed a new one! "Ella," he said suddenly, "do you know, I've been thinking it would be nice to have a family reunion here at the old place."

Aunt Ella looked surprised, but pleased, and said she thought it would be wonderful. The children didn't know exactly what a family reunion was but at least it was something new, and must be fun or the elders wouldn't seem so pleased over the idea. So they began asking questions, the answers to which were most satisfying, so their approval was assured.

"How would you go about it, David?" Aunt Ella asked after the chatter had subsided.

"Well, here's a surprise for you. Aunt Josie will be up Tuesday, for the balance of the week, and . . . . but the chatter had started again, so he had to wait for them to quiet down.

"Aunt Josie" was Aunt Ella's younger sister and lived with Grandma Harrington in Manchester, where Uncle David boarded during the week. She was a great favorite with the children and they were delighted and much excited over the announcement of her visit.

"Children! Children!" Aunt Ella finally exclaimed. "DO keep still a few minutes. I want to hear about the reunion, and can't hear a word while you are all talking at once!" So they quieted down, for they wanted to hear about it too.

"Well," Uncle David said, "we've been talking about it at Grandma Harrington's for some time, and we thought the best way would be for me to make out a complete list of the family, and write letters to those who live away from Goffstown. So Aunt Josie said she would come up this week and write the letters as she knew you would be too busy. Those who do live in town can be notified, and when we hear from everyone, we can decide on a date."

And so the arrangement was made, and the rest of the evening was spent in conversation about the reunion and the family.

Aunt Josie did come up, and wrote the letters, and several afternoons that week Pegasus was harnessed to the Surrey and they drove to the Village to talk things over with all the Paige's there. Everyone seemed enthusiastic over the idea, and finally the last Saturday in August was agreed upon as being the best possible date for the affair. Those who came from a distance could plan to stay over-night with several of the relatives thereby getting in a longer visit, and the men who farmed or had gardens felt that the work was about done as late as that, so they could best spare that day. Millie, as she told Uncle David, thought that date best because her father would be there then – "That is," she added, "if we're invited. 'Course we aren't really PAIGES – but I've been here so long I *feel like one!*"

He told her and Aunt Ella also, that they were invited, and he added, "And I tell you what we'll do. When everybody's here, we'll hold a meeting and just *adopt* the Rumney's into the family – how's that?" She replied that she thought it was just grand!

So all the rest of the summer they were busy as bees, with chores, play, berry picking, and much talk and planning about the Reunion. They were all on their good behavior – most of the time, although I am sorry to have to say that twice they slipped up – Bert and Millie being the culprits the first time, and all of them the second! I think those need chapters by themselves, for they are much too sad to mix in with the joys of planning a Reunion.

Chapter XI

One day, not long after that, the five older children were playing in the barn when Millie suggested they go up to the cupola. At first, the others did not seem to want to much, but she persisted, and after a while, up they trooped, gasping for breath when they entered the little place, for the windows were closed and there was not a breath of air. But as soon as they opened the windows the fresh west wind came blowing in and it was soon cool and comfortable.

They crouched on the floor looking out at the lovely scenes, except that Millie seemed to have something other than scenery on *her* mind. Bert studied her intently, wondering what was "brewing," but knowing that he would hear about it sooner or later if he waited patiently. Before long, tiring of "just looking out the window," as Flora said, she and Jennie departed in search of something more exciting, leaving the other three behind. Suddenly Millie startled them by saying dreamily, "I wonder what it would be like to look down into the yard from off the end?"

"End – where?" asked Josie, while Bert, who knew exactly what she meant, was speechless.

"There! Off the end of the ridgepole!" Millie explained, impatiently.

"My goodness!" came the reply. "I guess it would look funny all right, - only nobody could get out there to look."

"I could," Millie replied, calmly and confidently. Whereupon Bert recovered his speech, and said, "Well you couldn't, an' if you could you better not! Golly! If you slid off you'd go down three stories, an' break your neck!"

"Pooh! Who'd slide off?"

"You would, prob'ly – it looks slipp'ry as glass."

"Oh Millie, you *mustn't!*" Josie cried in anguish at the bare thought. "You couldn't walk out there without ---"

"Ain't goin' to walk," was the reply, opposition making her determined to try it "I'm goin' to sit down an' *hitch!*"

Bert, mulling the idea over in his mind, said, "Well, I s'pose you *could do that!*"

More terrified than ever that Bert would certainly do it if Millie did, Josie cried, "Your mother'd be scared to death, Millie Rumney, and so would mine!"

"What you goin' to do?" was Millie's retort, "Run an' tell 'em an' be an ole tattle tale?"

"Wouldn't be tattling if I told her before you did it." Josie snapped back "Mama says I'm the oldest, an' must use my judgment 'bout what's tattlin' an' what I *should* tell her.

"You're not older'n me, Josie Paige," Millie exclaimed wrathfully.

"No, but I'm older'n Bert, an' if you do it, he will, ----an' if he does it Flora will! And she began to cry, ----something Millie could never hold out against.

"Oh, all right then," she exclaimed disgustedly. "Come on, let's go down stairs an' play somethin'!" but she cast a wicked eye at Bert, and he knew the matter was far from ended.

Sure enough, later, when Josie was helping with the dinner dishes, and Jennie and Flora had disappeared, he got a signal and the two conspirators slipped out of sight.

"Let's sneak up to the cupola again," she said, "I'm goin' to try getting' out on that ridgepole."

"You better not. Honest, it *is* dangerous, Millie," he replied, feeling duty bound to try and dissuade her, but knowing very well he couldn't. To tell the truth, he hoped she would give up the idea, although it was a fascinating one!

"Well, what are *you* afraid of? You don't have to do it, do you?"

"N-No ---I don't have to ----but if you do it, I'm goin' to, too."

"Well, let's keep quiet. I dunno where Flora and Jennie are, an' we don't want anybody to know what we are up to."

So they tip-toed up the stairs and opened the cupola windows again.

"I won't go *way* out, but I'm goin' out a little way, anyhow," she said, as she looked out. It did look an awful distance to the ground, and Millie almost wished she had never brought the matter up at all. But she wasn't one to back down, although Bert would have been glad if she had.

She sat down on the window sill, her feet hanging out, and gingerly lowered herself to the ridge pole, a bare brown leg on either side of it, while Bert held his breath. And presently she began "hitching" herself along, as she had expressed it, until she was six or eight feet from the cupola.

"You there?" she questioned, not quite daring to look over her shoulder.

"'Course I'm here," he replied, "How does it seem?"

"Fine," she replied. "It's easy as pie! You comin' out?"

That was dare enough, and with a nonchalant "Sure," ---out he went! They sat there on their high perch a few moments, but having no audience, it soon palled, so they edged backwards, and sat side by side on the window sill.

"Would you really dare to go way out to the end?" he asked presently.

"'Course I would," was the reply. "It wouldn't be any harder to go way out than where we did go, would it?"

"You know what I was just thinkin'?" he asked. "I was thinkin' how funny it would be if we did it tomorrow when the Sewin' Circle was here!" and his dark eyes twinkled wickedly.

"Sewin' Circle? What's a Sewin' Circle?" his companion asked.

"Goodness sakes, don't you know what a Sewin' Circle is? Well, it's a lot of women b'long to our church, an' they all meet together an' sew for the missionaries, or the poor."

"Oh!" she exclaimed, "like the Womans' Guild in our church."

"I dunno, most likely. Anyway, Mama has 'em here once ev'ry summer, an' they sit out on the lawn an' sew. And they're comin' tomorrow."

"Tomorrow!"

"Ya-ah, I most always duck down to Frank's or somewheres, 'cause all they do is sit an' talk – mostly talk!" He grinned again, and added, "I bet it would scare 'em almost to death if we hollered to 'em an' they looked up an' saw us way up here lookin' over at 'em!"

"US!" exclaimed Millie, indignantly. "US! How could they – we couldn't *both* look over!"

"We could if I scotched down an' most laid on the ridgepole."

"Yes, - but where would I be?"

"Oh, you could kinda kneel down 'cross my back, couldn't you? Golly, all they could see would be two heads a-lookin' down at 'em!" and they both giggled at the vision.

For a while they sat there and talked it over, and then slipped innocently down the stairs to hunt up the others. But, it was understood that neither should tell anyone of their scheme.

Next day, immediately after an early dinner, they disappeared and were no where to be found. Josie was disconsolate at being deserted, and finally went off up to Elsie's with Flora and Jennie.

Aunt Nellie and Aunt Ella hurried to get ready for the coming guests, who soon made their appearances. Everything went beautifully – for an hour or so. The minutes of the last meeting were read, two letters also from absentees, cake and lemonade was served, and needles and tongues were flying.

Suddenly a loud "YOO-HOO!" broke a temporary silence. They looked up the road and down the road, toward the barn and toward the house, but it was not until another "YOO-HOO!" louder than the first was heard, that they looked _upward_! But at that last strident howl, every neck was craned upward to the barn roof.

Two heads, apparently bodiless, jutted over the end of the ridgepole – one directly over the other, and when every eye was focused upon this weird looking apparition, another "YOO-HOO!" from both throats at once, nearly split their ear drums!

It was several seconds before their mothers recognized the culprits. Aunt Nellie turned pale and Aunt Ella _felt_ as if she did. All the ladies shrieked, and one or two nearly fainted, and the two gargoyle-looking creatures on the ridgepole began to have serious misgivings as to the result of their prank!

Aunt Nellie, perhaps the most scared of all the on-lookers, was the first to recover. Anger added itself to fright, and her voice boded no good to her daughter when she called, "Millie, come right straight down here!" She, of course, did not mean _straight_ down- but Millie got the idea perfectly!

She inched off Bert's back, and both "hitched" their way over the ridgepole to the cupola as rapidly as they dared.

"Oh golly!" Bert exclaimed as they hurried down the stairs, "my mother is mad as hops! I bet I get strapped! An' your mother, - what'll she do to you?"

"Spank me most likely. She's a great believer in spankins', papa says. But they don't seem to do much good!"

"I'll tell you what we'll do," said her companion. "Let's run down the ramp like the dickens, an' go out through the barn yard. We can get across the brook an' hide – an' maybe they'll cool off. Don't make any noise now – come on."

But alas for running down the ramp! Or escaping! Or hiding till they "cooled off!" Aunt Ella, figuring on those possibilities, stood quite grimly, for her, at the tie-up door, and Aunt Nellie was right at the foot of the stairs – so the two criminals yielded to fate and gave themselves up!

Bert did not get strapped, but he would much rather have been than knowing he would have to wait in dread till Saturday, for his mother had said quietly, "Go over after the cows, Bert, it is nearly time. We will leave the matter of the ridgepole business for your father to settle."

Millie stood waiting her sentence. Her mother said in an icy voice, which belied her temper. "Go into the house." She went, of course, followed by her mother – at very close quarters! Oh yes, she got spanked as she had prophesied she would, but as she told Bert, "It didn't seem to do much good!"

Chapter XII

THE MYSTERY AT HARRY BROOK

They were grouped, panting, on Big Rock, recuperating after a strenuous tromp. Bert, Jennie, Millie, Flora and Josie. "Whew!" said Flora, "I wish I was over to the brook, so I could paddle my feet an' get cool!"

"Pooh! That wouldn't cool *me* much!" said Millie. "I'd like to be down at the river, and get in all over!"

"Me too," echoed Jennie.

"I'd like to be down at Harry Brook," added Josie, and there was another echo of "Me too," this time from Bert. And after a moment or two he went on, "An' after I'd get cool I'd like to do some 'vestigatin'!"

"Vestigatin' what?" asked Millie, idly fanning herself with her hat.

"The house. You know…" he went on, lowering his voice. "I b'lieve there's sumpin' mysterious 'bout that place."

His listeners were properly impressed, not only with the sepulchral voice.

"What you think it is?" whispered Josie, edging closer to him.

"I dunno," he answered, "But I'd like to find out. I bet there's sumpin' hid in that ole house, gold or jewelry- - -"

"Or maybe important papers," Millie put in, her mind already seeing the searching, and finding - - - "sumpin'."

"I wish we could find it," she went on. "Maybe we'd all be rich!"

"We couldn't find it without goin' in" Josie replied, logically, "An' we wouldn't dare do that."

"Who wouldn't!" exclaimed Millie and Bert as one.

"Well – I wouldn't," she returned with emphasis.

"Me either," said Jennie with full emphasis as much.

"I would - - if Millie and Bert did," said Flora who tried to emulate Millie in anything she did.

"It's no use tryin' to get in when we're down there on picnics," said Bert, "Cause Mama's there an' she won't let us!" And he shook his head regretfully.

"You couldn't get in anyway," remarked Josie, who someway felt that mischief was brewing and disapproved. "You *know* Frank tried the door last time we were down there an' it was locked, an' prob'ly the window is too."

"Maybe it ain't," said Millie hopefully if inelegantly.

"Well what I say, is le's go down and see if we can get in," said Bert, and the fat was in the fire!

There were gasps from Josie and Jennie, and nods of approval from the two tomboys, while Josie expostulated further.

"Why Bert Paige! You know Mama wouldn't let us go down there alone!"

"Pooh! What's goin' to hurt us I'd like to know! Nuthin', Nuthin' at all! Course she wouldn't let us if she *knew* it, but if we just went – she wouldn't know anythin' about it. We go over to the brook an' everywhere an' she never worries!"

"Course not" echoed Flora and Millie. "Come on, le's go!" And Flora added, "You'd better stay home Fraidy Cats," and the two 'conscientious Objectors' immediately about faced and determined to go if the other three did. Then they would share in the treasure they hoped to find!

So off they went, more or less hilarious on the long walk through the pastures, but growing gradually quieter as they reached the chestnut trees and came in sight of the lonely, desolate looking house. Even Bert and Millie and Flora ceased their chatter, but whether from a faint fear, or from "acting" I don't know. But it served to quite complete Josie's and Jennie's trepidation.

The place seemed absolutely silent. Nothing stirred except a bird now and then. Even the brook seemed quiet, hardly a gurgle or a ripple.

They crept nearer and nearer, but Josie stopped a few yards from the house, and Jennie stayed with her. The other three tiptoed on and up the three rickety wooden steps. Yes, the door was locked, just as Frank had found it. By standing on tiptoe, Bert could peek under the torn and lop-sided red curtain at the window, but there was only the same rusty stove and broken chair just as it had been before. They tried the window, but could not lift it.

There's another room out back," whispered Bert. "I can see light comin' through, so there must be another window. Come on, - le's go round."

So they crept through the tangle of bushes and nettles, round the house to the back. There was no back door and only a very small window, but as the ground sloped upward, they could easily reach it. And it opened!!! But the space was very small indeed, and Bert decided he could not possibly squeeze through.

"You can, though, Millie, - or Flora," he stated finally, after trying it himself.

Flora flatly and emphatically refused. "I'll go in if you and Millie do," she said, "but I won't go in there alone."

"Fraidy cat!" jeered Millie, who had hoped she would.

"Fraidy cat your own self!" retorted Flora, spunkily. "You don't dass go in yourself!"

"I dass too," contradicted Millie, and so picked up on the boast immediately.

"All right, smarty," was the reply, "Le's see you. I dare you to!" and Flora won, for Millie seldom refused a 'dare'.

So with Flora and Bert pushing and lifting, in she went, scared and trembling inwardly, but outwardly unconcerned, into the tiny room, plainly a kitchen.

"Go through a' see if the key is in the front door," whispered Bert, "an' if it is, let us in," and he and his companions started back around the house. Millie hastened to obey, for she was only too anxious for their company.

There was a key, but it was rusted, and it took some twisting before it turned in the lock. The door was swollen too, and it took the combined efforts of the three to open it, squeaking and squealing on its hinges. Millie breathed a sigh of relief as they entered, for she had had no liking for the dreary looking place all alone.

They went back to the kitchen, for, for some reason it seemed to be the most likely place for hidden treasure! A sad little room it was too, with fallen plaster and lathe showing, a small rusty cook stove and its sagging funnel stuck through a hole in the wall, and one rickety chair at a hinged shelf that had evidently served as a table. In one corner was a sort of cupboard, just three wooden shelves on which were a few dusty dishes and pans, and in another corner, a ladder-like affair, leading to the loft above. One look was enough, for it looked pitchy dark up there, and they could see through the open space that it was not over six feet from floor to ridgepole. It looked mysterious and forbidding, and no one offered to go up or asked another to go. A make-shift sink stood near the window, but there was no pump, so evidently water had been brought from the brook, or perhaps a well.

Gingerly, Bert climbed up on the chair and poked round amongst the dishes and pans on the shelves, and Millie lifted the stove lids and looked in the oven – but they found neither gold or jewels, or 'valuable papers."

Disappointed, they adjourned to the front room. Josie was standing at the door, poised to run if necessary, but Jennie still stood where they had left her – at a safe distance. Bert went over to lift the curtain so there would be more light, but at the first touch, down it came, rod and all. They all jumped at the noise it made, and jumped again, as Millie, standing near the stove, gasped and pointed at a big red stain on the floor! "LOOK!" She cried. "O-OH! Blood stains!"

Josie took one flying leap to the bottom of the steps, but Bert advanced – a little way, 'towards the discovery. Flora made a dash for him, clutching his arm, but he pulled away impatiently.

"MURDER!!" He exclaimed, in a sepulchral voice. "There's been a MURDER here!!!!"

With a squeal of terror Josie rushed over to Jennie, crying, "There's blood stains in there, Jennie There's been a murder!" and off they flew, hand in hand, to get still further away from the scene of the crime!

"Maybe the murderer's right here now," whispered Millie, with cold chills running up and down her spine. "Hiding up in the attic maybe."

"Ya-ah," Bert whispered back. "I guess maybe we'd better be getting' out of here," and the three went quietly but hastily toward the door, stopping to listen, but hearing nothing.

"Golly" Bert said, still whispering, "I s'pose we'll have to tell Walker we came in here. I dunno what he'll say!"

"I don't care what he says," said Flora despondently. "I'm wonderin' what Mama'll say! Oh dear, I wish we'd stayed home where we b'longed," and her voice sounded near tears.

"I – I s'pose we ought to shut that back window," Bert said looking at Millie hopefully. But Millie wasn't having any.

"Well, go shut it then," she returned firmly. "I wouldn't go back out there for a million trillion dollars! My goodness, maybe that ole murderer is comin' down that ladder right this minute. Who's goin' to get in the window anyhow? I had to squeeze through!."

"Nobody, silly," replied Bert. "Only skunks might, or rats or snakes."

"Well, let 'em then," she returned, "Who cares 'bout ole skunks an' rats an' snakes?"

And at that they stayed not upon the order of their going, but went pell mell through the door, although Bert did stop long enough to pull it to. And then they ran to join Jennie and Josie, and all five fled, not stopping till they reached the chestnut trees.

"Let's stop here an' get our breath," gasped Bert. "We can see the house from here, an' if the ole murderer comes out we'll run again. He couldn't catch us from here, anyhow."

"He could me!" wailed Jennie, "an' prob'ly Josie too! We're too fat to run fast as you can!"

"Well we won't leave you anyhow. He wouldn't dare follow us up near the road," replied Bert comfortingly.

"He would too," she returned, half crying. "Nasty ole murderers dass do anything! It's all your fault anyway, Bert Paige, wantin' to find gold an' jewelry!"

"Oh hush up, for goodness sake," snapped Millie. "You didn't' have to tag along did you? Prob'ly he's sound asleep up in that attic, anyhow!"

They did not stay long, soon starting for home, with frequent looks behind them, but no "murderer" appeared. They debated, pro and con, as to confessing what they had been up to, Jennie and Millie as 'cons,' Bert favoring telling Walker, who owned the old McCoy place. He felt that some one older should know about the murder and the bloodstains, and that perhaps the miscreant was still hiding in the attic – and he knew he ought to tell of the 'house- breaking,' and leaving the place open for further invasion. Flora rather sided with Jennie and Millie, but Josie closed the subject with decision.

"You can tell Walker or not," she stated, "but I'm goin' to tell Mama. We've been bad, - bad to go down there without askin' her, and badder to go into the house. I s'pect Walker could have us arrested for doin' that," at which Jennie and Flora wailed, and Millie and Bert looked frightened. "He prob'ly won't," she went on, relenting, "But Mama'll punish us some way - but I'm goin' to tell her just the same.

"Oh, all right – I guess that's what we better do," admitted Bert, "I'll go with you when we tell her – but I'm goin' to tell Walker too."

"An' *I'll* go with you too, Josie," said Millie, her voice quavering. "We'll all go, won't we?" and Jennie and Flora nodded solemnly.

After quite a few minutes of silence at the prospect ahead of them, Bert suddenly remarked, "Say, you know, I been thinkin' bout somethin' awful queer. That door was locked when we got there, an' the key was inside. Walker musta locked it – but how did he get *out*?" No one seemed able to answer – so there was another mystery!

When they reached the house, they filed silently into the house and into the sitting room, standing in a line in front of Aunt Ella, who was mending. She studied them gravely, knowing quite well that something was in the offing! But she said nothing at all, which of course made it just that much harder for the children.

Josie gathered her courage and said, after a moment, "M-Mama, - we've been bad."

"You have?" her mother replied trying not to smile at the five anxious faces. How bad?"

"Not so awful bad, Mama," Bert put in hastily. "An' it was my fault. I suggested it."

"Oh, - you suggested it?"

"Well, but we *all* did it, Aunt Ella," Millie said not willing Bert should take all the blame. "We all did it, only Josie and Jennie didn't want to, - much, - an' they didn't do the baddest part, either."

"Well, it's very nice of you and Bert to take most of the blame. Now supposing I hear the whole story. Josie, perhaps you had better do the talking."

Josie shifted her position and cleared her throat, which somehow seemed quite dry, although they had stopped at the well for a drink before coming in.

"Well," she began, "we went down to Harry Brook, - not to the brook exactly – but to the house. We – we wanted to go in---"

"What for," her mother interrupted. "You've looked in the window, - I have myself, and there's nothing to see."

"No, but we thought there was hidden treasure there, so we went in."

"She didn't go in, Mama, or Jennie either," Bert put in.

"Well, I went to the door an' looked in," Josie replied. "An' I guess I'd have gone in if I hadn't been too scared."

"Jennie stayed way out in the field," Millie added.

But Jennie was not going to let the others take all the blame either so she said bravely. "I was scareder than Josie! But I *wanted* to go in."

"You all seem anxious to confess your guilt and let the others off," Aunt Ella said quietly. "But let's not bother with who went in and who stayed out. How did you *get* in?"

"Through the window in the back room," Bert replied.

"I did---I got in," confessed the culprit.

"I helped her – I pushed," from Bert.

"Me too," this time from Flora.

"An; then I went an' unlocked the door, an' let Flora an' Bert in. They couldn't get through the window.

And then the story rushed through to its ignominious end, first one talking, then another, sometimes all five at once. Aunt Ella seemed to get the gist of it, although it came in sections, and she had a hard time keeping a sober face.

When at last they stood silent, waiting for the ax to fall, as it were, she said quietly and calmly, "Well, no matter who instigated –er- started this escapade, or who went in or who stayed out, you are *all* old enough to know that I did not want you down there alone. And you certainly know that you have no right to enter another person's house without permission. I really don't think this is anything very *dreadful* that you have done, but I think disobeying me and entering Walker's house deserves some sort of punishment, - and something that will punish all of you. So I think we will just not go down to Harry Brook again this summer."

"No picnics down there – even when you are with us?"

"No picnics, so I am punished too."

"Not even when Papa comes up?" exclaimed Millie.

"Not even then. Now run along and play till supper time."

"Can I go down to Walker's?" Bert asked, anxious to have it over with.

"Certainly. Go right now and tell him just what you have told me."

"But Mama! You haven't said a single word about the *murder!*"

"No, I haven't, have I. Well, my dear, I don't think there ever was a murder at the McCoy place. That's Walker's business anyway, so run along and tell him."

Bert went off down the hill, and the four girls, rather subdued, went over and sat down on Big Rock, to await his return, and to talk over their punishment.

Walker and Jim were sitting out on the bench beside the barn door when Bert appeared. They listened, gravely at first, but finding it more and more difficult to remain so, as the tale unfolded.

"Millie got through that back window?" Walker exclaimed. "Why, my grief, it only opens about eight or nine inches! That young one is like an eel! Some day she's goin' to slip and slide right down a snake hole!"

And a little later he interrupted again. "Blood stains! You don't say!"

But by this time Jim was laughing uproariously. "That winder broke the time we had that wind storm last fall. Blew half the winder curtain down an' the rain soaked it an' made them stains. Them ain't blood stains Bert!" and Bert didn't know for sure whether he was relieved or sorry.

Walker explained that when they had found the window broken they had put in another old one they found in the barn, and then locked up the place again.

"I been thinkin' 'bout you lockin' it up Walker," said Bert. "The door was locked on the inside though – so how did you get out?"

"Oh,- well, we couldn't make the key turn on the outside, so Jim locked it on the inside an' crawled out the window- the *front* one though, an' then we nailed that – so the place was all shut up tight. You'd ought to have tried the *back* window, Jim," and they both laughed again.

"I'm sorry 'bout goin' in, Walker, an' 'bout leavin' the window open an' the front door unlocked. I did shut the door, but tramps or skunks or sumthin' might get in through the window."

"Well, I don't believe they will tonight, Bert. Jim and I'll go down tomorrow and fix it so nothing ever can get in. I've been meaning to for some time. It's all right, no harm done, so you just forget it."

So Bert tore up the hill, much relieved, to tell the girls all about it, while Walker and Jim went in to regale Mrs. Little with the story of the hunt for treasure, and the bloodstains.

Of course the children did not get to Harry Brook again that summer, but on their very first trip down the next year, what was their surprise on reaching the Chestnut grove, to look down and see no house or barn! Not a trace of them was left except a few boards piled up off to one side. So Walker had done what he said he would, "fixed it so nothing can ever get in."

Yes, the old house and its mystery, it's bloodstains and it's "murder" was gone forever, but Harry Brook was still there, singing it's same old song, rippling and gurgling – just as lovely as ever.

Chapter XIII

M y, but Reunion week was a busy one, so busy that Millie and Josie had no time to grieve over the parting that was to come the following Monday. Everybody worked like a beaver, indoors and out. The shrubs had to be pruned, the lawn mowed and raked; the barn was swept till not a spear of hay showed, and the windows were all washed. The house, of course, was swept and garnished, dusted and polished to a fare-you-well, as Bert said.

And there were more "chores" than ever in the house, for Aunt Ella was cooking, cooking, cooking! Dozens of doughnuts, plain, chocolate and jelly filled; dozens of cookies, sugar, cream, molasses and ginger! Pies! Cakes! And the last two days, beans and meats baking, hams and corned beef boiling, pans of biscuits and loaves of bread – white and brown!

Aunt Ella knew there would be a good many present on Saturday, and though all the local Paige's would bring food as well as glass, silver and dishes, she intended to be prepared for any number and to have a well filled larder.

But everybody helped, Aunt Nellie, and the girls, and the men saw that the wood box never got empty. The children got down long-unused dishes and glasses from high shelves and washed and wiped them. They polished silver, cracked nuts, chopped raisins, beat eggs, and did it willingly. It fact, it was fun!

Josie wrote a special poem, Millie reviewed a recitation, Jennie and Flora learned new songs and a duet, for both were sweet singers, for it had been decided to have an entertainment, and everyone had been notified, and asked to help if they could.

Uncle David announced that he had given up his work in Manchester and was going to be at home hereafter, running the farm, something he had long been planning to do. So he was busy, perhaps busier, than all the rest. He and Uncle Lyman and Bert made saw horses and long tables from lumber left from building the barn, so long that they filled one side from end to end. And they made benches, so that with the lawn settees and chairs, everyone could be seated. Yes sir! Everybody worked *that* week, and oh, how they all hoped for a pleasant Saturday.

The day before the Reunion arrived – what a surprise! Even Aunt Ella knew nothing about it. The two uncles had seemed rather restless, even stopping their work several times during the forenoon, to stand in the barn door and gaze down the road. And a little after eleven, Joe came driving up the road with the big farm wagon, with whatever was inside covered by a big tarpaulin. He drove straight into the barn, but when the children attempted to follow, they found their way barred by Uncle David, and the door closed – right in their faces! They didn't quite dare to slip around and come up the ramp, for he had shaken a finger at them and said, "No admittance for ten minutes!"

It was a long ten minutes, but at the end of it, Joe backed out of the barn, waved at them and drove off toward home, grinning. These queer goings on had been reported by Josie, and Aunt Ella thought nothing unusual, - and then – suddenly---WHAT a commotion!

There on the left stood a brand new piano! A lovely black upright piano! There were cries of "Papa!!!" "David!!!" "Uncle David!!!!" And then everybody talking at once till one would have thought they were at the Tower of Babel!

Josie said the least, but her eyes were shining, and she was gently rubbing a hand over the polished woodwork. "Well Josie," her father said, after a moment or two, "Want to keep it? How about sending Bertha back and keeping the piano, eh?" Everybody laughed, even Josie, but she leaned against his shoulder and replied, "No sir! If we can't have 'em both, we'll keep Bertha."

After they had quieted down a little, he explained that he had unloaded it in the barn because of the entertainment next day, and that Joe and Jim Hazeltine would be up Monday and help move it into the house.

Next day was perfect! Not a cloud in the sky, and not too hot – a wonderful day for such a gathering. There was a mad scramble to get an early breakfast out of the way and the chores done. The three aunts, for Aunt Josie had come up for the occasion, covered the table with white paper from a roll Uncle Lyman had bought. Josie and Millie placed plates and cups and saucers, and Jennie and Flora set the glasses about, each with a folded paper napkin inside it. A rope of evergreens was laid completely round the table just inside the plates, and in the center space were sugar bowls, cream pitchers, and low dishes of flowers. Later, of course, "the eats" as Bert expressed it, would be added.

By nine o'clock the Village Paiges began to arrive, in order to help. There was Willey Paige in his surrey, with Uncle Isaac and Aunt Jane, his pretty wife. Susie and their little girl Zetta, and in his buggy, his sister Lottie Dow and her husband.

Frank Paige with his wife Josie, yes, there were three Josies there, and their son, Guy. George and Hattie Paige, with their three children, Nat, Will and Lena. Charles Richards and his wife and three little girls, Gertrude, Minnie and Grace, and his sister, Nell. And Ed Kidder and his wife and three children. From then until nearly noon, the "Out of Town Paiges" arrived, Jonas Paige, who was Uncle David's Uncle, the Pattens, the Pecks with their three children, Mable, Edith and Olive, all from Manchester. Uncle Frank Paige from Keene, with his wife, and two daughters, Minnie and Myrtle. Aunt Sarah Barnes, with her husband and three girls, Effie, Edna and Myra! It was quite a gathering! And a merry one.

The men folk inspected the farm and new barn while the ladies divided what time there was between visiting and putting the finishing touches to the dinner and dinner table, while the children romped and played and got acquainted and reacquainted.

Somehow, no one knows *just* how, impromptu committees were appointed for the afternoon, Aunt Ella and Susie Paige to see to a program, Uncle Frank and Will Paige to see to contests and games for the youngsters, and Uncles Isaac, Frank and David to conduct a sort of family meeting or conclave.

Finally the loud ringing of the old school bell which was kept at the farm, called them all to dinner – not that anyone needed calling! The ambrosial aroma of coffee, baked beans and meats had already drawn them all yard wards, where they had been "champing at their bits," as Uncle Isaac said. Uncle Jonas as the eldest Paige, and Uncle David as Host were seated at the head and foot of the long table, the rest just anywhere, as it happened. After the coffee was poured and served all sat down, for they had arranged to have everything on the table, ready to be passed from hand to hand.

The table certainly looked not only sumptuous, but beautiful, - that is to say, then they sat down, but when they had finished – well, it was sad looking to say the least.

After the diners could not take another bite or another swallow, they sat back to chat and recover from the effects of such a repast. But finally the word "to work!" came. The ladies, most of them, hied kitchenward, to attack the pile of dishes, which the children brought them, that being their duty. And the men took down the tables and saw horses and stored them to one side. They carried the benches outside and put them facing the barn door, which was to represent the stage opening, evidently. Then they pulled the piano forward – and their "chores" were done.

In less than an hour, for "Many hands make light work," you know, dishes were done and sorted out, and the food put away, so out the workers came to fill out the audience.

The children's contests were about over, potato races, a three legged race, egg in a spoon race, and they were finishing a peanut hunt, one wrapped in a dollar bill!

When at last the happy winner was showing her lucky find, the seats filled, and everyone settled down to listen to the entertainment. Bert did his famous jig, for his chum Frank had been invited as a special guest and, of course, had his harmonica with him. Uncle David was as much surprised at his son's terpsichorean accomplishment as Aunt Ella had been at the famous picnic. Then Frank played and everyone sang a few songs. Jennie and Flora sang, with Aunt Josie presiding at the new piano. Most of the other children spoke or sang and everyone received plenty of applause. Millie recited her new piece, suddenly transforming herself into a fat-stomached Dutchman names Hans, who told them about trying to put a setting of eggs under "mine vife's leetle plue hen". He stood up on a barrel, and the head of the barrel broke through and down Hans went, tight in the barrel! His wail of "Undt all de nails go down aundt I couldn't coom up – de nails sticker me all aroundt!" simply convulsed her audience. Uncle Frank never missed a reunion and never failed to beg to hear about Hans each time.

It had been decided that Josie's poem was a fitting end for the program as it was very appropriate to the day. She came forward with very pink cheeks, but she read it clearly and distinctly, so that everyone heard every word.

THE PAIGE REUNION

Dear friends, we welcome you who've come
To see once more the old Paige home.
We welcome you with might and main
And hope to a reunion again.

We wish all the Paiges of old could be here.
But I'm sure we feel that they all are near.
And loving us all as we love them.
I'm sure they are smiling and saying "Amen!"
This poem doesn't tell you half I would say
To all of you, friends, this Reunion Day.
But there's one thing you're thinking
Of that I'll engage – You're thanking your stars because
You're a Paige!

There were shouts of acclamation and gales of laughter, and Josie was quite the star of the program.

After they had talked it all over and had quieted down, Uncle David rose and made a short speech. He asked if they did not think it would be a good idea to hold an annual reunion, perhaps on that day, the last Saturday of August, as that seemed convenient for everyone. There was loud and unanimous approval, so he went on, proposing to organize, in a way, electing a leader, and a secretary to take notes of the "doings" as he expressed it, and read them the following year.

This too, was heartily endorsed, so he proposed Uncle Jonas as leader, being the oldest Paige, but Uncle Jonas thought someone in Goffstown, and preferably one living on the old place should be in charge, so Uncle David was elected then and there. Susie Paige was elected as Secretary, and began at once taking notes.

Then 'Young Frank" as he was called, to distinguish him from the other Frank, suggested, not a fee exactly, but a sort of offering. "There is always, more or less, expenses connected with this sort of thing," he said, "paper, envelopes, stamps, etc. And I herewith give a dollar each for Josie and I." Uncle Isaac said he though that a very sensible proposal, and added his offering to Frank's, as did the others. Uncle David then rose and said he had not thought of that, but so long as it was in order, he would like to make another suggestion. "I think it would be fine to have a stone, one off the place, engraved appropriately, inscribed to the original Paiges who settled here. What do you think?" Everyone seemed to think it a splendid thing, so he went on to say, "I think I know of just the stone – it's over near the pines, and it seems to me a good place, for it would be right there in the triangle, between the main and Centre roads. Why not have a dedication service next Reunion? It seems to me it would be a fitting way to show our respect to our forebears, and as Josie said in her literary offering, "I'm sure they are smiling and saying Amen!"

The rock that still sits at the top of Paige Hill reads as follows:

Erected By Descendants of JAMES PAIGE
Who Emigrated From England 1750
Benjamin, 2nd
John G., 3rd
Isaac J.
John F., 4th
David A.
1910

There was steady and long applause, and much talking it over. Uncle David finally interrupted again to say, "I have one more, <u>very important</u> proposal to put before you. It is important to us who live here on the hill, and to a certain young lady here, - eh, Millie?"

Millie jumped when she heard her name, and was a little abashed to find every eye on her, and everyone smiling. But she knew what was coming, and wriggled with excitement. She hadn't forgotten the "Adoption' promise, but had been afraid he had, and in her joy to find he remembered, she stammered, "Y-Yes S-Sir!"

"When Ella and I first talked over the idea of a Reunion, Millie was afraid she and her parents might not be invited to attend. She said, "I know I'm not really a Paige, Uncle David, but I've been here so long I *feel* like one!" And he laughed as he recalled her serious face, - and so did everyone else. "So I move herewith, that Mr. and Mrs. Rumney and their daughter Millie be adopted into the Paige Clan, and that they are invited to attend Paige reunions as long as they are held. Those in favor, please say "Aye!'"

I'm sure the Gilmores and the Littles must have heard that "Aye," – and there were no "Noes."

There were Paige Reunions for nearly forty years, although there are none held now. But the stone, with its inscription, still stands in the triangle, and over it, a huge maple, that was planted as a small sapling, at the dedication, still stands guard.

Chapter XIV

There was the usual hubbub at the breakfast table one lovely July morning, although if anyone had been particularly observing, they would have noticed that Bert had very little to say, seemed to have less appetite than usual and seemed singularly restless.

"Come, children," said Aunt Ella, as she began clearing away the dishes. "Stop your chattering and finish your breakfasts. Remember, the Sewing Circle meets here this afternoon, and I have a lot to do."

"Isn't there something I can do to help?" asked Aunt Nellie, wiping egg yolk off Millie's chin in spite of wriggles and protests.

"You might dust the parlor and sitting room if you will," Aunt Ella replied, "although most likely they'll all want to sit out under the trees. They generally do, especially if it is very hot."

"Well, it certainly promises to be hot today. I'll be glad to do the dusting, and I'll give Bertha her nap when the time comes. "MILLIE!!! Will you hold still a minute! My goodness, you've got egg almost to your ears!"

"Well, I can't help it," Millie returned, still wriggling. "I was just takin' a mouthful and Flora jiggled my arm."

"I did not," denied Flora. "You're always twistin' round so you can see ev'ry thing at once, and you turned your head just as I –"

"That will do, Flora," interrupted Aunt Ella. "You'll *all* have to help a little this morning, I guess. Josie, I wish you would make a batch of sour cream cookies. I've made cupcakes, but a good many prefer cookies, and yours are always nice and crisp. Jennie, you will please do the breakfast dishes –"

"Then Flora's got to wipe them," Jennie put in hastily, for she hated to work alone.

"Sorry, but Flora will have to keep Florence amused and out from underfoot," replied her mother, but was interrupted by Millie, who said quickly, "I'll take care of Florence, Aunt Ella." She well knew that her mother was ready to suggest that she help with the dishes, but she much preferred being out of doors, hence the speedy offer. But she had another and more cogent reason, for she had caught Bert's eyes, fixed on her with a steady, unblinking stare for some minutes past.

Now she and Bert had a secret code of communication, which plagued and puzzled the other children. They had figured out a few of the minor signals, but had been unable to decipher any of importance. The steady stare had informed her that there was something very special in the offing – mischief of some sort probably. And when he saw that she "got" the meaning, his head canted backward and a little to the left, which indicated they were to meet in the barn. Then when his heavy eyebrows started twitching spasmodically, she knew it was something VERY special, and she had no wish to be delayed by dishes.

She knew Florence would not disturb the conference in the least, for she was a quiet little mouse, and easily kept amused.

Aunt Ella felt relieved, now that things were all lined up, and she hurried off to her own occupations. Bert drifted barnward, apparently chore-bound, and presently Millie and Florence wandered past Big Rock, with doll and doll carriage. But once they turned into the pasture road, Bert appeared from under the barn, and he and Millie perched themselves on a rock for a little chat, apparently, while Florence contentedly wheeled her doll carriage up and down nearby.

"Golly," exclaimed Bert, "I thought you'd *never* catch onto my signals! You ate an awful lot of breakfast, seems to me!"

"I did not!" contradicted Millie, indignantly. "I only ate 'bout half my oatmeal, an' besides...

"Oh well, never mind," he interposed, anxious to get at the business on hand. "I've got the wonderfullest plan! You'd never guess what it is! We can do it this afternoon an' have the most fun! I bet we can scare those sewin' circle women most to death!"

"HO!" Millie exclaimed, disparagingly, "I bet we *can't!* My mother hasn't forgotten what we did last year, Bert Paige, an' neither has yours! We can't do one single thing this year 'cause they ain't goin' to let us even be here!"

"Huh!" he returned loftily, "Who wants to be here anyhow? I wouldn't stay round their ole sewin' circle, an' listen to all those women gassin' an' gossipin' – not if you'd pay me. Where you goin' to be if you can't be here?" he went on, curiously.

"Oh, my mother went an' said she thought it would be nice if Jennie and Flora an' me went up an' spent the afternoon with Elsie. An' your mother thought so too! My mother can think up the worst things! It wouldn't be so bad if Josie was going to, but she's got to stay home an' help serve the cookies an' lemonade. You'd think two grown up people could do that without makin' Josie help!"

"That's all right 'bout goin' up to Elsie's" said Bert. "We can play the trick all the easier. Last year was fun, - but this time! Oh Golly!"

"Well, what is it?" questioned Millie, impatiently, anxious to be let into the secret. "I bet it won't be *half* as much fun as last year. "Member all those women 'most faintin' away when they saw us out the ridgepole?"

Both of them broke into paroxysms of laughter, making so much noise Florence paused in her walk and smiled in sympathy, although she had no recollection of last summer's prank.

When he could speak, Bert replied, "Oh yes, it will – it'll be ten times funnier-"

"An' prob'ly I'll get spanked ten times harder'n I did last year," returned Millie, adding dismally, "Most likely Mama'll use the hair brush this time." Bert shook his head sympathetically, somewhat taken aback at such a prospect. "That's right. Prob'ly we'll both get licked this time. Mama doesn't use the strap very often – but I bet she will this time!" And then he added, desperately, "But I don't care if she does. It's the best joke I ever thought of, and ----"

"Well, what IS you ole joke, anyway!" she demanded, and then, well knowing that she would be expected to take an active part in whatever it was, she suddenly queried, "an' what will I have to do?"

Bert wriggled himself into a more comfortable position, and proceeded to divulge the great scheme. "Well….I was up to Joe's this mornin' just before breakfast, an' he showed me a black snake he'd just killed in the hen yard. Golly….but it was a whopper! I asked him if I could have it, if I'd bury it, an' he said sure I could."

Millie looked at him disgustedly. "What you want to bury an' ole black snake for --- an' what's the joke to it, an' what's it got to do with the Sewin' Circle, I'd like to know! Oh, I know – you was goin' to lay it out on the lawn to scare 'em! Pooh! I don't think THAT'S much of a joke! They'd all know it was dead, most likely!"

"Oh, is that so, Miss Smarty!" exclaimed Bert, angered at this cool reception. "Why don't you keep still a minute an' let a feller 'splain! Who wants to leave it on the lawn! Here's what les' do," and he proceeded to unfold his plan, whispering and gesticulating. Millie listened attentively, her grin growing wider and wider, now and then interpolating a suggestion or a criticism, but it was quite evident that she had changed her mind about the "Joke."

Ten minutes later Bert disappeared into the barn to attack the belated chores, and Millie turned and gave her undivided attention to entertaining Florence. And presently Jennie and Flora appeared, and proposed a trip to the brook to see if there were any baby turtles sunning themselves.

But Millie had duties to perform in connection with the afternoon program, and wanted to get away by herself for a while. So she said "You go ahead and I'll be over in just a little while. I want to see if Josie has got the cookies done. Maybe she can come too."

For a wonder, there was no opposition, and no one volunteered to accompany her, so while the three went down the pasture road, Millie very quietly and nonchalantly sauntered across to the lawn and the house. The sedate walk and silence would have been enough to cause suspicion and possible investigation had she been seen, but it happened that no one was in sight, so she went unmolested.

She slipped through the front door and across the sitting room without a sound. In the top drawer of the sewing machine, she found what she was looking for – a large spool of strong linen thread. She reeled off several yards, wound it round a bit of paper, and pinned it carefully inside her pinafore pocket, and then like an Indian, she slipped out noiselessly. Closing the door, she went flashing round to the side door with her accustomed whoops and leaps.

She longed to confide in her chum, but Josie was a good little girl, and would very likely have felt that she must discourage such a naughty caper – perhaps ever warn her mother. So Millie hugged her guilty secret to herself and kept silent.

Somehow the long forenoon passed, an early dinner was eaten, Florence and Bertha put down for their naps, and Millie, Flora and Jennie set off for Elsie's, leaving Josie looking longingly after them.

The ladies of the Sewing Circle began to arrive, and Bert dutifully put horses in the barn, or tied them to trees and the hitching post near Big Rock, and brought out more chairs as needed. But when the last team was taken care of – he disappeared as silently and suddenly as mist before the sun! He slipped out the North door and by a lengthy detour arrived back of Joe's barn. There he climbed a tree and brought down a pasteboard box, well hidden among the branches, and from it carefully removed a very dead black snake! He handled it with no apparent repugnance, stretching it out on the ground and gazing at it admiringly. If you ask ME – it certainly was a horrid looking thing!

For a while he amused himself in one way or another, until Millie arrived. She had slipped away from her companions, during a game of hide and seek, having considerable trouble in evading Flora's keen eyes, but eventually succeeding.

After inspecting the snake, she removed the black thread from her pocket and gave it to Bert, who tied one end securely round the snake, just back of the vicious looking head. For some time they worked together with suppressed giggles, putting the last touches to their nefarious scheme.

Joe noticed them from the barn window, but could not make out just what they were doing. He felt fain forebodings, but being inured to their escapades, he contented himself with muttering, "Wonder what in tunket them rapscallions are up to!"

In the meantime, fourteen ladies were seated on chairs and settees on the sun dappled lawn at the Paige's, with needles and tongues briskly busy. Cookies, cakes and lemonade had been served, and Josie was wondering if she dared slip away and run up to Elsie's. But just before she made up her mind to risk it, one of the ladies, happening to glace up the road, remarked, "Here comes Bertie, and I guess it's your little girl with him, isn't it, Mrs. Rumney?" Aunt Ella and Millie's mother looked a little surprised at seeing those two together and coming toward the house so soon, but made no remarks.

The children were about half way between the two houses, just at the beginning of the long pile of cord wood between the road and the stone wall, when Bert dropped behind, apparently picking and eating wild raspberries that grew rampantly all along the road. But Millie kept straight along, and they could hear her singing away in perfect serenity. Suddenly, however, Bert yelled wildly and dashed toward her. "A snake!" he cried. "A snake! RUN Millie, RUN!" And began picking up and throwing stones – but being careful not to hit the snake.

Millie gave one look behind her, let out a war whoop that no Indian ever surpassed, as if in mortal terror. With arms flailing wildly she started running – and straight for the lawn and the Sewing Circle!

Six or eight feet behind her, with now and then a vicious leap a foot or more off the ground, was a long black snake, apparently making every effort to attack the flying little girl! And to those fourteen ladies it was a fearsome sight! They could not, of course, see the black thread, but they certainly *could* see the snake and the look of horror and fright on both children's faces.

Bert had grabbed up a stick, and with great heroism (so the ladies thought) was belaboring the snake. All was going by schedule except for one slip up! The loop of thread round Millie's finger was *supposed* to be slipped off before she reached the lawn, whereupon Bert was *supposed* to kill the already very dead snake! But alas! The loop simply refused to slip, so the snake breezed right along behind Millie!

The shrieks of those ladies far surpassed those of the two children. Chairs and settees were tipped over, except one or two on which terrified women stood with skirts held high and tight around their legs! The others stayed not upon the order of their going, but scattered in all directions, some for the house, some for the barn, and two who ran for and fell over the stone wall between the lawn and Little's field!

ALL BUT AUNT ELLA! She had been suspicious from the first, so she stood her ground until Bert, Millie and the snake reached the edge of the lawn. She had seen Bert's face and knew there was no real terror in it, and that his dark eyes were shining with wicked glee, and that in spite of his blood curdling yells, he was grinning broadly. And a second later her keen eyes discovered the tell tale black thread.

And in that second, Bert realized that his mother was not in the least frightened, - but that she *did* look distinctly annoyed! The grin vanished from his face, the yells ceased abruptly, and the mischievous look in his eyes changed to one of apprehension. He braked to a sudden stop, his course veered, and he made for the barn. He dashed through the tie-up, down the ramp, out into the pasture, and did not once stop until he had crossed the brook. It was almost time to drive the cows up, anyway! He felt a twinge of compunction at leaving Millie to face the music alone, but he felt sure that his presence would not hinder or alleviate whatever might be coming to her, so he slowly went on to the back pasture.

Millie too, had stopped when the ladies had scattered, and stood wrestling with the recalcitrant loop of string. One by one, the ladies came down from their perches, out of the house and barn, and over the stone wall, as they saw Aunt Ella push the snake aside with her foot. Each reacted according to her disposition, some laughing, some scowling, some muttering balefully, but they were as one in the opinion that those rapscallions should be punished severely. They needn't have worried.

Aunt Nellie had been one of those who had sought sanctuary in the house, and when she came out, from her expression, Millie wondered if the game had been worth the candle! Red flags of anger and embarrassment were showing in her cheeks, and sparks were in her dark eyes. "Millie Rumney," she said, after she and Aunt Ella had made apologies to the other ladies, "March yourself into the house and go up stairs. Undress yourself and go to bed, - and I don't mean in Josie's room. In MY room. I will be up shortly!"

Bravely Millie walked away, but there was considerable trepidation in her heart, and she though of Bert's prophesy – "It'll be ten times more fun than last year!" and of her reply.

She found Josie awaiting her in the front hall. "Oh my goodness, Millie!" She exclaimed, "Whatever made you do such a thing, and after what you did last year, and the spanking you got! Oh dear! I bet you get a worse one this time!"

"I bet I do, too – an' with the hair brush pro'bly," was the stoical reply to her Job's comforter. "But I don't care – not very much. I had a bushel of fun, anyway!" And with a giggle at the memory, she added, "Did you see 'em all skedaddle?"

"Course I did, I skedaddled, too. I bet you would have skedaddled yourself, if you'd seen somebody running right towards you with a big black snake after'em! My goodness, it looked 'bout as big as a boa constrictor!" Then she added hastily as she happened to glance out doors, "You'd better hyper up stairs right this minute, 'cause those women are gone an' your mother's headed this way. Here, here's some cookies I saved for you," and she thrust a paper bag into Millie's hands. "You better hide 'em somewheres cause she'll pro'bly make you go to bed without your supper."

"Goodie! Thank you, Josie. See you in the mornin' – Bye," and she 'hypered' up the stairs.

Let us draw the curtain on what happened that next half hour, and to Bert in the woodshed a little later on! But dear reader, if you think it cured them of dreaming up further escapades – well, as children say, "You just wait an' see!"

Chapter XV

W hat a lark! Aunt Ella and Uncle David were going to Manchester tomorrow, to spend the day and next night with Grandma Harrington, to celebrate her birthday. And they were to keep house all by themselves, that is during the two days! Aunt Ella didn't think they were quite old enough to be alone in the house at night, so Emma Phillips was to come down in the evening to stay. They did not mind that, however, for they all liked Emma, and she knew lots of games they could play.

They had been told that they were under Josie's supervision, and all had promised faithfully to "mind her." Aunt Ella felt that Josie was young for so much responsibility, but she was trustworthy, and very capable. Millie, although a few months older, was not nearly as mature, and was full of mischief, but she was one to respond to trust and confidence, and loved the younger children devotedly. Aunt Ella knew she would stand by Josie through thick and thin. So she took her to one side, and told her how she was depending on her to help Josie with the others, and that she was put "on honor" not to be naughty or play any pranks during her absence. Millie, proud to be so trusted, promised earnestly to "be good ev'ry minute," and help Josie all she could – which eased Aunt Ella's mind a good deal.

Aunt Ella had been rather nervous at the idea of leaving them, for it was the first time she had ever done so, but Uncle David pooh-poohed her fears saying that if they never had a chance to try it they'd never learn to stand on their own feet, so she finally decided to go.

The next morning, Joe arrived early to take them to the train. The children gathered on the door rock to wave good-bye, and watch them out of sight. They had been thinking how wonderful it would be to be all alone, "on their own" as it were, for two whole days, but somehow, as they drove off down the road they felt a queer sort of emptiness, and they were very quiet when the carriage had actually disappeared round the school house curve! Suddenly Florence's eyes filled, her lips puckered, and she wailed, "Mama! I want my Mama!"

But Bert grabbed her and rolled over and over on the grass till the tears stopped and she shouted with glee, crying:"Do it 'gain, Bertie, do it 'gain!" till he was completely out of breath.

They all laughed at the antics, and presently Josie hopped up, smoothed down her pinafore and said, "Well, come on, let's get the breakfast dishes done, and the beds made, and then we can decide what we're going to do."

Whereupon Bert replied, "Huh, I <u>know</u> what <u>I'm</u> goin' to do," with such a supercilious air that Josie was irked into answering caustically, "Well, Mr. Smarty, you can't do *anything* till you get your chores done!"

"Pooh!" he replied, "I know that without you tellin' me. I'm goin' to drive the cows over, an' clean out the tie-up room, an' fill your ole wood box chock-a-block full, an'<u>then</u> I'm goin' fishin' with Frank."

"Won't you be home for dinner?" asked Millie almost wishing she did not feel that she must stay with Josie, for she loved fishing too.

"Nope," he returned, airily. "Helen's goin' to put us up a lunch so we won't have to come home."

"Where abouts you goin' to fish?" she continued, only to get another airy reply. "Oh I dunno, - somewhere's round. If we get any, maybe I'll bring some home for supper."

"Well, you needn't," interrupted Josie. "I'm not going to get a hot supper. Mama said I needn't. So if you want fish, you'll have to wait till dinner tomorrow."

"Pooh, I don't care," he replied. "Maybe Frank an' I'll cook 'em this noon, an' maybe we won't get any anyhow." And off he scampered to get his barn chores done, while Josie gathered up the reins of government.

"Jennie, you wash the dishes, and I'll clear the table and put the food away."

"I'll wipe 'em, Jennie," said Millie, hastily, "and I'll make the beds so we can get through and start playing." She led the way into the house, doing a cake walk, and singing, "Oh, them Golden Slippers," so lustily, that they all joined in, and Flora and Little Florence behind her, tried to imitate her cake-walk.

But just before Jennie started the dishes, they came near having a quarrel, for Flora came out with a pan of garbage, and being full of mischief, she held it out toward Jennie, saying, "Here you are Jennie. Empty this and I'll start the dishes."

"I won't!" exclaimed Jennie, angrily. "You just empty that yourself, Flora Paige! You know very well it makes me sick every time I go near that ole pig barrel!"

Now it was a fact, it really did make her sick, and Aunt Ella had long ago excused her from doing it, but children love to tease and for a long time they tried in all sorts of ways, to make her do it, from quarrels to bribery. The latter had succeeded *once*. She got as far as the barrel, but was sick then and there, and they had stopped bothering her.

Josie intervened before a real quarrel started by saying, "Flora – you stop your nonsense! You know Jennie can't stand doing it, so you just march out there and do it yourself."

"Fuddy-duddy!" Flora exclaimed. "I don't care. I don't mind emptyin' the ole swill or feedin' the ole pigs either! Jennie's just an ole silly!"

"Maybe she is, but you empty it yourself – an' you know Mama says we should say <u>garbage</u> – not swill."

"Well, when she's here I'll say garbage – but today it's SWILL!" and having the last word and a loud one, she flounced out.

In a short time the work was done, and they went out to the rock to make their plans, finding Flora already there, and all over her "huff". As I look back, I often wonder that that old, rough door rock didn't have five or six dents in it; so many small posteriors were so often planted on it!

Josie started in at once, for fear some of the others would propose some amusement that would side-track what she had in mind. "I thought we could go berryin' this forenoon," she said, "an' get a few for supper with crackers an' milk," and then seeing the complete lack of enthusiasm in the faces of her audience, she added hastily, "an' maybe a few more, - just enough for a pie for supper tomorrow night. Mama an' Papa love blueberry pie, an' I could bake it in the morning." She felt pretty sure they would relent, for they all loved to please the absentees.

"I thought we were going to have a good time today!" Jennie said, pouting a little. Millie too, could think of a lot of things she'd rather do than pick berries, but as usual, she stood squarely behind Josie.

"So we can have good times today," she exclaimed, "Huh! It won't take very long to pick that many berries! Josie's an awful fast picker, an' there's four of us! After we get enough we can play all day."

Josie smiled at her ally, and seeing that Jennie was partly convinced, she said, "No, it won't take long and we'll just go over to the South swamp, 'cause Florence couldn't walk too far. Bert says there's lots there. We could take our dinner over instead of coming home, an' play over in the pine woods afterwards, or go to the brook."

All the sulky looks vanished, for they loved picnics. They all ran in and made sandwiches and packed two shoe boxes, Jennie drew a can of cold water, and Flora collected pails, four five pound pails and a gill cup for Florence. They all went out but Millie, who locked the front door on the inside and skipped through the Buttery and out "Jack's hole," in the shed door, - and off they went.

The berries were plenty as Bert had said they were, enormous silvery blue ones, and high bush berries are easy to pick, so long before the noon whistle blew at the Village, Josie's pail was heaping full. Jennie's and Flora's were about half full, and Millie had about a quart in her pail, and goodness knows how many in her tummy! Florence, being too small to reach them had filled her cup with acorns, but no one disputed it with her when she called them 'bu- berries.'

By that time it was getting quite hot, so they crossed over to the pine woods, and were glad to reach the shade and coolness, and sprawl out on the thick satiny carpet of needles. Once cooled off, they made short order of the lunch, and then, while Florence had a nap with her head in Josie's lap, they played "My brother came from China," and "Animal, vegetable or mineral." An hour or so later, they idled back along the wood road, stopping to paddle a few minutes in the brook.

When they reached the yard, they flopped down on the grass, and Josie stretched out in the hammock, for the walk from the brook is sunny, and they were hot and tired. But after a while Josie noticed that Jennie was picking one fat berry after another out of her pail, so she said, "Jennie, you go in and open the doors and we'll go in and wash up."

Jennie was still tired, and she was getting so fat she could hardly squeeze through Jack's hole, so she answered snappily, "I don't want to. Go do it yourself!" They all laughed because they knew Josie couldn't possibly get through, and she said sharply,

"You know well enough that I can't get through there. I'm fatter than you are and you can't hardly do it. Now you march right along!"

"Won't!" returned Jennie. "Let Millie do it. I'm tired."

"Is that so!" said Millie. "I'd like to know what you've done to make you so tired! You never lugged a thing back 'cept your own pail of berries, an' that wasn't half full!"

"Well, you didn't have half as many as I did, so there!" Jennie sputtered.

"Maybe she didn't," Josie put in, "But she lugged one of the boxes and the can too!"

"Pooh! Ole empty can – didn't scarcely weigh anything! My legs ache, too!" she whined, trying to look distressed.

"Growin' pains," returned Josie, callously. "Anyway, you go along in there an' open the doors, Jennie Paige, or I'll tell Mama."

"Go ahead an' tell her, tattletale," muttered Jennie, but never-the-less, she started toward the shed. Stooping, she put her head through the opening, but made no move toward wriggling through. Instead, after a second, she backed away and dashed for the others with such an expression on her face they stared at her in amazement.

"Animal!" she gasped, clutching Josie, who had jumped from the hammock. "Animal! There's a great big animal in there!"

"Jack, prob'ly" replied Josie calmly, although a little doubtfully, for she knew Jack would have come bounding to meet them the moment they had gotten in hearing.

"Tisn't either Jack!" Jennie denied, shivering in fright.

Millie was looking at her skeptically. "You can't fool me, Jennie Paige," she cried. "You just want to make me go in and open up, but I won't, so there!"

But Josie interrupted. "No she doesn't Millie. She did see something - I can tell by her looks. Oh dear, what will we do?" And she shook Jennie off and picked Florence up.

Millie began to feel a little frightened too, although she was still suspicious. She hated to think she might be getting fooled, but she couldn't go back on Josie, who was really scared as she could plainly see.

"I don't care!" she exclaimed. "I don't believe she saw one single thing! My goodness, if there was any ole animal in there it'd be out here by now, after us," at which both Jennie and Flora began to cry. And even Josie seemed near tears. It wasn't the tears so much as Josie's courage in picking Florence up and holding her, ready to run with her, that braced Millie into action. "Oh, Fuddy Duddy!" she exclaimed. "Stop your crying! I'm goin' to see your ole animal myself!" and with that she marched off, head up and outwardly calm, but with inward trepidation. In spite of herself, she went slower and slower as she neared the shed, but inevitably, she reached it, and stooping down, peered through the small open place.

There was an animal there, lying right at the foot of the Buttery steps, - a brownish animal, head on forepaws, and it's green eyes glaring straight at her!

In thirty seconds flat she was back with the others, and herding them toward the front door. She pushed and shoved them along, whispering excitedly, "Go on! GO ON! Get up on the door rock an' don't make a sound. I'll run an' get through Bert's window an' let you in. Go on, I tell you!"

She left them there, huddled round Josie, and flew silently round the side of the house, and yanked at Bert's screen till it came out. Tumbling in, she stopped long enough to close the window, for fear the creature in the shed might be prowling round and get in, and then she ran through the house and opened the front door. The four terrified children crowded in hurriedly, and closed and locked the door behind them.

Josie leaned back against the door a moment, studying Millie intently. She knew Jennie had seen something in the shed, or genuinely thought she did, but she wasn't so sure about Millie! *She* was always "up to something" pretending to faint, or be drowning, or pretending to have a grass snake in her pinafore pocket and chasing Jennie, scaring her half to death. So naturally, she was a little suspicious now. After a moment's intense scrutiny she said, "Millie, did you really and truly see an animal out there? Or are you fooling us? You know you promised Mama you wouldn't play any tricks."

"I know I did, Josie, and I haven't, cross my heart. I truly did – a great big one, truly." And Millie's reply was so fraught with alarm that Josie was *almost* convinced.

"All right," she replied, "But all the same, I'm going out there and see for myself!" and out she marched.

Millie shooed the others into the sitting room, crying, "Now you stay right here with Florence and Flora, Jennie. I'm going with her," and then she nearly finished poor Jennie by adding, "You stay till somebody comes to rescue you, if Josie and I never get back!"

The wails of the three were ringing in her ears when she reached Josie, who was well on her way back to the house by this time, and as they dashed into the house, she exclaimed, "There is something there! It's a great big lynx an' it was lookin' right at me! Oh Millie, what'll we do?"

They all crowded together in the big arm chair, Florence and Flora in Josie's lap, and Millie and Jennie on the two arms. They debated as to what they should do.

Should they get Uncle David's shot gun that hung on the wall over his bed, or his revolver that lay on the top shelf of the Secretary, or Bert's sword? Maybe they'd better have all three handy! Maybe the gun would be best, if they could creep out and shoot it, - but who would do the shooting? And could they hit it? Supposing they missed it, what would it do to them? Fortunately, they decided against the idea, for neither gun nor pistol was loaded!

Perhaps they could all go to the Buttery door and scream and pound and stamp and scare it off! But it was such a vicious looking creature they were afraid it wouldn't be scared enough to go away, besides, it might be asleep and would be mad if they woke it up! Not knowing what it would do – jump right in one of the windows, prob'ly an' kill them all! Oh dear, what were they to do. And then, an awful thought occurred to them. What if Bert came home and went right into the shed?

"Oh dear," Josie said, "I wish Walker or Jim would go by for their cows. We could holler out the window an' they could shoot the ole thing dead!"

"Tain't near time to go for the cows," returned Jennie, pessimistically, "an' they wouldn't have a gun anyhow."

"N-no, that's right" said Josie, and she was very close to tears.

"Why don't somebody run down to Walker's an' tell him," asked Flora, and Josie gave her a big hug.

"Oh, my goodness, yes!" she cried. "Why didn't we think of that right off? Who'll go? I can't run very fast, an' I guess I'm too scared to run at all! MILLIE!!! Millie – you go. You're not so scared as I am, an' you can run awful fast. You can beat Bert some times. You go!"

Millie hesitated, but her spirit of bravado was roused. Hadn't Josie said she wasn't as frightened as she was? Even if she was, Josie didn't think so. And she could run fast. Besides, everybody would think she was awful brave if she went. But aside from these thoughts which flashed through her mind, she really wanted to do something – hadn't Aunt Ella *trusted* her? So she got up and went to the door, reluctantly, but she went. "All right, I'll go," she said, "I don't 'spect I'll never get there, but I'll run like the dickens. But you all watch out the side window, an' if that ole Lynx comes out of the shed, you holler an' bang on the window so he won't notice me an' chase me. I bet he can run faster'n I can!" And her voice trembled at the thought. They promised faithfully to do so, and with a "last good-bye" look, she opened the door quietly, slipped out, and crept to the corner of the house. There was no sign of the intruder, so she flashed across the yard and down the hill. Never, *never* had she run so fast! She certainly would have beaten Bert that day! Her bare brown legs pistoned up and down, her arms flailed like those on a wind mill, and her hair blew straight behind her as she flew along. She did not pick her way either, but tore along regardless of pebbles and small rocks, - in a straight line for Walkers. The children, peering from the side window, entirely forgot to watch for the Lynx, so intent were they on the marathon runner. But the animal did not appear – he was apparently waiting for some victim to enter the shed!

Walker and Jim were sitting in the barn doorway, cooling off with a pitcher of cider, after unloading a rack of hay, when they heard racing steps turning off the road into the yard. A breathless voice called, "Walker! Jim! Walker!" in such terrified accents that it brought both men to their feet.

Millie came tearing up to them. "Oh Walker!" she cried, "Jim! Come QUICK! Get a gun and come quick! There's a great big lynx in our shed!"

"A what?" exclaimed Walker, staring at her doubtfully. He knew Millie's penchant for jokes, - in fact he had been the butt of one or two – and he much doubted a lynx being anywhere near the neighborhood. Still, the terror in her face looked genuine, and he felt that there must be *some* reason for it.

Jim had risen at the word lynx and had gone into the house, coming back in almost no time at all, with a gun over his arm.

"How do you know it's in the shed?" Walker asked, still a little skeptical. Millie, gaspingly, told of starting to crawl into the shed. "I saw it, Walker, honest I did. I looked right at it - he was awful big – he was most as big as me!" And then as Walker smiled broadly, she added "An Josie saw it, too."

That changed the looks of things immediately with him, for he knew Josie was no "prankster," and he started toward the road.

"Come on, Millie," said Jim, as she stood watching Walker. "Come on. We'll go git the ole critter." And he held out his hand for hers. But she still held back. She knew that the other children would be safe now, and she had no desire to go back herself, until the lynx was shot.

"I-I g-guess I'll go in an' v-visit with Mis' Little a while," she stammered. But Jim only laughed and said, "Why I can't get through that dog hole in the shed door! You'll have to git in and lift up the hasp so's I can open the door. Then you can run for the house if you want to. Come along," as she still hesitated, "Walker'll be getting' there, an' he hasn't got a gun. Critter'll be a mile away if we don't mosey along."

So, reluctantly, she "moseyed" along, and they caught up with Walker just as he turned into the yard. "You sure you can hit him?" she asked as they neared the shed.

"Guess so," he replied calmly. "I most gen'rally git what I aims at," and she felt a little safer. Then as they reached the shed door he went on, "Now git along in there quicker'n scat an open the door, an' then skedaddle, if you want to."

Shaking in her shoes, she went in, as he had bade her,' except that she *didn't* "skedaddle." She was in and the door open in a split second, and Jim was inside and the gun aimed so quickly she couldn't have gotten out the door, let along skedaddle! So she stood spellbound, fingers in both ears, eyes closed.

The animal was still there by the steps, eyes glaring, motionless. But there was no shot. Millie opened her eyes, to see Jim staring at the "critter," and not even aiming the gun! And in another moment, to Millie's horror, he walked straight up to it and contemptuously stirred it with his foot!

Just then, Walker and the four children, who had ventured to come out when the reinforcements arrived, appeared in the door. Jim stooped and picked the creature up by the tail and held it aloft, his eyes meeting Walker's.

"Quite a lynx!" the latter said, calmly, shaking his head. "Quite a lynx – only it's a dead one! And not quite as big as you, Millie." And then, as Jim tossed it to one side, both men broke into gales of laughter.

"Pooh!" exclaimed Josie, suddenly. "Tain't a lynx at all! That's only a little ole woodchuck!" And then, as the men were still laughing, her eyes flashed and she went on angrily, "I don't care if it is only a woodchuck! We *thought* it was a lynx, an' I think Millie was awful brave to run way down to your house. It looked awful big," and her eyes filled with tears as she added, "an' we was awful scared!"

Walker put an arm round her and said, "I expect you was Josie, an' I don't wonder at it, either." And then he added a bit of philosophy, which was a way he had. "You see, Josie, bein' afraid makes things look bigger an' worse than they are sometimes. Millie was plucky to come after us, an' you just remember to always do that if you get scared." After being profusely thanked by the children, he and Jim went off down the hill to regale Mrs. Little with the tale.

The children were seated on the lawn and about recovered from the afternoon's fright when Bert came home, with Jack trailing wearily behind him. Breathlessly, the girls started telling him their adventure, all talking at once, and rather mixing things up. But when they got to peeking in the shed and seeing the "Lynx," he hooted wildly. "Ho, ho, ho!" he roared, "LYNX! You thought it was a Lynx! Why, my gollie's Frank an' me saw that ole woodchuck down in the garden eatin' the cabbages, an' we sicked Jack onto him. They had a awful fight, an' Jack got bit on his nose – but he killed the ole critter. An' we slung it into the shed so's we could skin it tonight! LYNX!" he repeated disgustedly.

He listened while they went on with the rest of the story, staring at the two older girls with neither disgust or ridicule on his features, and when they finished, he said respectfully, "Well, my goodness, you was both pretty brave all the same, thinkin' all the time it was a lynx an ' a live one at that!" This was praise indeed and the girls were highly flattered at such a tribute from Bert.

As Uncle David and Aunt Ella listened the next evening, they too praised the girls for their courage. "I knew I could trust the younger children with you," Aunt Ella said with an arm round Josie and Millie. And Uncle David nodded and said, "I told you you could!"

And that is the story of the Lynx that was "Most as big as me!"

Chapter XVI

One of the favorite games for after supper playing was "hide and seek." Quite often Mabel and Frank would come trudging up the hill, and Alice and Elsie down the road, for Paiges was a sort of half-way place, and with so many already there, there was plenty of fun to be had. Almost invariably, someone would suggest, "Let's play hide and seek," and there was never a dissenting voice, - so a line would be formed, and someone would "count out" to decide who should be it. "Eenie, meenie, minie, mo,

Catch a darky by the toe,

If he hollers let him go,

Eenie, meenie, minie, _MO!"

Whoever was "MO! was "it" There were strict rules, and no infringements allowed. "It" must stand close to the big maple that stood almost before the front door, faithfully hide his eyes, and count by fives, to two hundred – and not too fast either, while the rest flew in all directions to get hidden before the dread two hundred was called.

The hiding had to be out of doors, except that one could stand behind the open barn door – but that was too easy, so it almost never happened. When "It" located a hider, both raced for the maple, and if "It" reached it first the other was "tagged," and obliged to be "It" next time. But if the hider was lucky enough to reach the tree first he was safe.

It was surprising how many places there were to hide oneself, and near enough to be able to get back to the goal quickly. Under the clump of lilacs, flat in the rhubarb or horse radish beds, back of the north door steps, behind trees or the wood pile – oh there were lots of places.

Best of all, they loved playing it when Millie's father was there during his vacation, for he was always ready to play himself, and often got the other grown-ups to join in, and the more the merrier.

Besides, he was fun. They all declared he must have Indian blood, for he could lie flat on his stomach, face hidden and his coat collar turned up to hide the white shirt collar, and inch his way along the grass without a sound, suddenly clutching someone by the ankle! Such squeaks and squeals you never heard, although they knew perfectly well who it was!

One evening, before anyone had suggested the game, they were all sitting on the front lawn, some on the grass and some on the door rock, just "visiting." In some way they got to telling Ghost stories, until finally, most of them were shaking in their shoes, even though not one of them believed in ghosts. So most of them were relieved when someone proposed the usual game of hide-and-seek.

For the first few games, Millie hid in one of her favorite spots, close to the stone wall at the end of the yard, flat on her face on the ground. The grass grew tall enough to hide her and she could see the whole yard, so when the chance came she could scamper across the yard to the maple and cry "safe." But after a while, she was afraid some one might have seen where she came from, so she decided to change her hiding place.

No one had seemed to notice that Uncle Lyman had not shown up between the last two or three games, but there were so many playing one would hardly be missed. Bert happened to be "It," and Millie was determined that he should not catch her, and she whispered to Mabel, who chanced to be beside her, "Come on Mabel! I know a *dandy* place, - and he'll never find us and we can tag in easy." The instant Bert started counting off she flew with Mabel close at her heels.

At the opposite end of the yard, near the corner of the Centre road, there was an apple tree, small, but large enough to make a good hiding place. Mabel stumbled over getting hold of the lower limb, so Millie gave her a "boost," whispering, "Hurry, he's almost counted out!"

She scrambled up just in time, and as Bert happened to go in the other direction they laid themselves out flat on two limbs, well hidden by the leaves. They giggled as they saw Bert creeping toward Millie's last hiding place and she whispered, "I knew he'd caught on to where I was, but he'll get fooled this time."

It was a lovely night, brilliant with moonlight, so bright that Elsie and Josie got caught almost immediately. The two girls watched, waiting for him to creep round the corner of the house, so they could make a dash for the maple.

Suddenly, Mabel said in a low tone, her voice quavering, "Millie, Millie, LOOK! What's that coming down the road?"

It was white and so were two long arms – or were they wings, spread out from its sides, and waving slowly up and down! Whatever it was, it was more than half way down from Joe's, much too near to suit the two girls. When it reached the end of the woodpile, and still kept coming, they recovered from the paralysis, Millie bent on the house and the protection of her father!

"It's a ghost, Mabel," she said huskily. "It's a ghost! Come on, let's run for the house," and she flopped down out of the tree, ready to run, but waiting for Mabel, who had been on the limb under Millie's and should have reached the ground first. Millie whispered angrily, "Lan' sakes, Mabel, don't be so slow – it's almost here!"

Just as she was about ready to reach up and yank her companion out of the tree, there was a PLOP! And Mabel landed on the ground in a little heap – and didn't move! Millie had been frightened enough at the "ghost" but this frightened her even more, but without even a look at the coming apparition, she tried to pull Mabel to her feet, but she did not stir. The "ghost" had reached the edge of the triangle and stopped there, still waving the long arms, and Millie with one final shake at Mabel's recumbent form, let out a piercing scream. "PAPA! PAPA!" she yelled, "Mabel's dead or fainted or sumpthin'. Quick PAPA-----SOMEBODY!!!!!"

There was an immediate commotion, I can tell you. Aunt Ella and Aunt Nellie, who had been sitting on the door rock enjoying the fun, came running toward the tree, and the children came from all directions.

The "ghost" dropped its white garments and made a mad dash across the triangle – and to Millie's amazement and relief, it was her father. He knelt down quickly, and with Mabel's head on his knee, took charge immediately.

As she had passed the well, Aunt Ella had grabbed up the pail, which fortunately was half full, and with her handkerchief, was bathing Mabel's face. Mabel declared afterwards, she hadn't really fainted away, but had been so scared, she couldn't stand or speak, let alone run, so she had flopped down where she was, and waited for whatever her fate was to be!

Poor Uncle Lyman was so conscience smitten, and solemnly begged everybody's pardon, that he was freely forgiven. Some of them even wished they had seen him, and tried to get him to get back into the rig again, but he positively refused. Aunt Ella declared she was as much to blame as he was. "I helped him" she said. "I hunted up the old sheets, and two canes to make his arms look longer."

Aunt Nellie sputtered and scolded, winding up with "No wonder Millie is always up to something! You're forever setting a terrible example for her, Lyman Rumney!"

But presently they were all laughing as he told how he had slipped out the North door and cut across Moore's field to get up to Gilmore's, falling flat twice, being hampered with the long skirt-like robe, and the two canes. By the time he had finished, even Mabel was in gales of laughter, but when it came time for her to go home, Uncle Lyman decreed that she was not to go alone. He, and any of the others who wanted to go, would see her safely home, which certainly relieved her mind, for she still felt a little shaky.

So Bert and Josie, Frank, Millie and her father walked up the road with Alice and Elsie, gathering up the "ghost's" discarded raiment when they came back, and then went down the road with Mabel and Frank. They sang and laughed all the way, so that by the time they parted at Pecoy's, Mabel was completely herself again.

But Uncle Lyman promised them that although he might play tricks on them sometimes, it would never be anything that could frighten them. "To tell the truth," he said, "I never dreamed anyone would really be SCARED tonight. I thought the minute they saw me, they'd immediately shout, "Pooh, that's no ghost – that's only Uncle Lyman."

Chapter XVII

"Who's goin' to the Ball Game today?" asked Bert, addressing the usual assembly at breakfast.

"What ball game?" returned Jennie.

"Why, just THE ball game," Bert answered, gazing at each girl in turn.

"Oh my goodness!" Josie exclaimed, "I forgot all about it! They planned it before school closed – the idea of my forgetting it!"

"Who's playing?" Millie asked, leaving Bert's question still up in the air.

"Oh, mostly the seniors, a few outsiders are playing against the New Boston High School. And now, if you've finished *askin'* questions, maybe somebody'll answer mine!" and with that devastating sarcasm, Bert sat back and glared at them.

"I am, if Mama'll let me," answered Josie, not at all alarmed at the glare.

"Me too," quoth Millie, even less so. She was no baseball enthusiast, but if Josie was going, so was she. Seldom did anyone suggest "going" without her immediate "me too."

"Then I'm going too," piped Jennie.

There was a groan from Josie, and an echo from Millie, but Jennie stuck her chin out obstinately and scowled.

"Oh for goodness sake, what do you want to go for, Jennie? You're only in the last grade in Grammar School, and these are seniors playing!" Josie said, cuttingly.

"Pooh, you're only a junior yourself – what do you want to go for?" returned Jennie.

"You won't like it anyhow. You don't know the bat from the ball, I bet. I bet you don't know baseball from ….."

"I do so, Josie Paige! There's nine players in baseball, an'…."

Everybody laughed, even her mother, who said, "Oh Jennie, don't be so literal!"

"I don't care!" Jennie replied, sulkily. "I *will* go. I'm goin' if Josie an' Millie do, so there! I can go, can't I, Mama?"

"Well, since you finally have asked me, I don't see any reason why not. It's a public affair, isn't it, Josie?"

"Yes, its public, Mama. The school voted to have a game once a month this vacation, to raise money for new uniforms," she replied, and then turning back to Jennie, "an' it costs ten cents to go. You got ten cents?"

Jennie turned up her nose, disdainfully and replied, "Yes I have got ten cents, Miss Smarty! I've got lots *more* than ten cents, too. I've saved almost all my blueberry money." And then, smirking and preening and stroking her hair, she went on, "I don't go buying new blue hair ribbons every week or two 'cause "blue looks good on my red hair," so's to make the boys look at me, - like some folks I know!" She stepped hastily out of reach as she dealt this devastating blow.

For a second Josie was staggered, and her cheeks reddened as everybody, even her pal Millie, laughed. She knew they had heard her make the remark Jennie had quoted, and she felt rather foolish. But she recovered quickly, and turning up her nose, retorted with emphasis, "No, I 'spose you haven't. By and by, when you get old enough so's the boys will even notice you, you'll be buyin' *pink* ones, 'cause you've only got common *brown* hair!"

"She only wants to go 'cause we're goin' anyway," Millie put in, rallying to Josie's aid.

"I know it," Josie answered. "Always taggin' along, slippin' after us an' listenin' to everything we say!"

Bert, who had been taking in this dialog with great interest, grinned and added his bit. "Listening to what!" he exclaimed, and then answered his own question disgustedly. "BOY TALK, prob'ly! That's 'bout all I've heard lately! I dunno what's got into you two lately, anyhow! You used to be some fun an' had a little sense, but by Crikey, you don't do hardly anythin' now but whisper an' giggle all the time. I wish't I hadn't asked who was goin' an' started all this fightin'!"

"Who's fighting?" Josie demanded angrily.

"He is," snapped Millie, realizing that Bert's "you two," had included her in his arraignment, and angry at this defection. "He's always…." But Bert had slammed the screen door and was gone.

Aunt Ella, who had been listening with an amused smile, rose and started gathering up the breakfast dishes. She sent Jennie out to look for eggs, and told Josie and Millie to do the dishes, thus separating the combatants long enough for the ruffled plumage to smooth down. She paused long enough, on her way to the kitchen to say, "Josie, when the dishes are done, you will please make the beds, and Millie, you had better write to your mother. You can mail the letter in the village this afternoon – provided you all behave well enough the rest of the forenoon to be allowed to go."

This veiled threat sufficed to produce exemplary conduct, and no further allusions to the matter were heard. "But she'll go – she'll tag right along with us – you wait an' see!" whispered Josie, as she started the dish washing.

Aunt Ella understood children pretty well, and felt that this feud was just a temporary phase. She knew too, that there was justifiable irritation on both sides. The two older girls were almost of an age, and had been inseparable from the first, but until lately, they had included the younger children in their play. Now they seemed to want to bar them out, and naturally Jennie resented it. It was aggravating of course, to have her persist in trying to be with them every minute, yet, of course, just as aggravating to her, to be barred out. "But it will pass," she thought to herself, "just as all their tantrums pass."

The game was not to begin till three o'clock, but by one, dinner was over, they were excused from doing dishes, and off they went to get ready. Bert galloped off to get Frank started, and a little later the three girls started down the road, Indian file, and keeping well to the sides so as not to get their shoes scuffed or too dusty. The two "chums" seemed to have no confidences to share, so Jennie walked serenely behind them, completely over her "huff."

The ball games were held on the Fair Grounds, across the river, and it was a long two miles and half walk in the heat, but luckily they got a lift just before reaching the Village, and right to the Fair Ground.

They were considerably surprised to see Bert and Frank seated in the Grand Stand as they entered. "Who gave you a lift?" Josie inquired as they passed them. "Nobody," Frank replied, and then at their mystified looks, went on, "River's low, so we crossed over on the rocks, an' all we had to do was climb up the bank an' cut across." No wonder they had arrived first!

Some of the Goffstown team, with it's satellites of admiring younger boys, were out on the field tossing the ball about, for it was still early for the game. Quite a crowd was gathered in the Grand Stand and on the bleachers, mostly young folks, but with a smattering of older men and women.

The girls had joined a group of schoolmates, Nattie Bell who was Josie's school chum, Mabel Pecoy, Blanche Whipple and others. Jennie felt a little out of it at first, but was enjoying herself immensely, and no one made her feel "shut out."

Presently the old stage arrive, bearing the New Boston players, accompanied by several wagons all loaded with excited and boisterous New Bostonites. The onlookers seated themselves in the Grand Stand, not far from our group, while the team joined the other players for a little "warming up."

"Oh my, just look at those New Boston uniforms! Don't they look nice!" exclaimed Josie. "And our boys in those old ones – some of 'em in *overalls*! I wish they had the new uniforms."

"Huh!" put in Bert, "uniforms don't win ball games, silly! We'll knock 'em higher'n kites – see if we don't!"

"I know that, silly yourself," returned Josie. "All the same I wish they had the new ones."

"Looks like they'd make money enough today at ten cents a person, to get 'em, with what they've got already," said Frank. "I call this a pretty good crowd," and he started trying to take count.

Privately, Millie was thinking that the New Boston visitors were better looking and more "up to date" than the home boys, but for all that she staunchly hoped the home team would win.

It was the custom then, to play three innings, and then have a fifteen minute intermission for collecting the admission fees. Today, at the end of the second inning, the score was tied. Suddenly one of the New Boston girls jumped up, and began urging their crowd to cheer their team. It was no practiced, rhythmic directing, as cheer leaders do today, but at any rate it sufficed to wake them up and they responded bravely.

The Goffstown support had been rather weak, too, so when Millie saw the response from the opponents, she bounced up, ran down in front of the stand, and apparently in a spasm, jumped up and down, yelling at the Goffstown supporters like a Comanche Indian!

"COME ON – COME ON YOU! WHAT'S THE MATTER WITH YOU? GOT SORE THROATS? BACK UP YOUR HOME TEAM – COME ON NOW! THREE

CHEERS FOR GOFFSTOWN!" And believe me, she got response! Everybody laughed and clapped, and what was more to the point, cheered lustily.

The players out in the field stared in amazement to see the Goffstown crowd on their feet, waving and cheering, with a small girl in front of them – apparently in a frenzy!

"For Pete's sake!" exclaimed Fred Dubois, "who's that dancing dervish out there? What's the matter with her!"

"Oh that's the Boston girl that boards up to Paige's summers," replied Will Pritchard. "Ain't nuthin' the matter with her,' cept Ethel Topliff says she thinks Goffstown's the greatest place on earth."

"Huh! Well, if she thinks that – there's sumpthin' the matter with her all right. She must be crazy!" For Fred thought it rather a dull place himself.

One of the other boys, the smallest on the Goffstown team, was William, or Bill as he was generally called, - Morgrage. He was in Josie's class in school, but living in the Village, he had never got really acquainted with her till she began going to High School. He knew who Millie was, but had never met her, and somehow, maybe because she was from Boston, he had always had the impression that she was a little "uppity," as he called it, - "Just one of them city girls, all airs!"

But she hadn't acted very "uppity" or "airy" today, and somehow his opinion moderated considerably. "Why," he thought, "she might be fun if you knew her!" And she sure had been comical prancing round and waking up the crowd!

The team was still staring at her when Dubois took up the conversation where he'd left it. "Boarder at Paige's, huh? Well, she's mighty homely, Boston or no Boston, that's what I think!"

"To bad!" said Bill, turning away and tossing the ball up and catching it. "She'd prob'ly feel real bad if she knew you thought so! Come on, fellers," he added, "Third inning."

A little later he was on first base. The batter hit the ball and started for first, and Bill shot away to second – to third- and home – and made it by sliding the last six or eight feet.

"Who's that boy?" Millie asked, and Mabel Pecoy, who was sitting beside her, replied,"That one? Oh, that's Bill Morgrage. He's in Josie's class at school."

He was trotting back to the bench, and as he passed in front of the Grand Stand, for they were still cheering, he made a sweeping bow, with a burlesque wave of his cap.

"He's a cut up, isn't he!" Millie remarked, and to Josie's horror, she rose and returned a sweeping curtsey, and then yelled at the top of her lungs, "HOORAY FOR GOFFSTOWN – AND FOR BILL MORGRAGE!"

There was laughter and clapping from the crowd and Bill grinned and waved to her before moving on to sit with the players at the bench.

Dubois, who had been watching this performance, slapped Bill on the shoulder and said, "Ha, ha boys! Bill's made a hit with Boston! I wonder how he does it?" and the boys all laughed.

"Ya-ya," returned Bill, "it's my beautiful face that does it," and he twisted round and dug his shoe into the sand, in mock bashfulness.

"All the same," said Dubois, "Homely or not, I bet she's lots of fun. She's got plenty of ginger anyhow."

"Bert Paige is in my class at school," piped one of the younger boys who were hanging round the team, "an he says she's 'bout as gamey as a boy. He says he can't hardly ever stump her, an' she has some new stunt 'bout every darn time she comes up here. She ain't afraid of anythin' either."

"Pooh, I bet anybody could scare her if they tried," Fred returned. "Anyhow, I dunno but I'll take our team some evenin' an' go up to Paiges' an' get acquainted." There were hoots and groans from the group but Dubois disregarded them.

Bill had been listening with a broad grin, and had groaned with the rest, but didn't say a word. Mentally he decided he would not wait for "some evenin'" to "get acquainted" but would manage to do so in some way, that very day,

In the meantime, Millie and Mabel had gotten into an argument, which was no uncommon thing for them. Once they had settled back into their seats, Millie had remarked; "My, but that what's-his-name can surely run! I'd just love to run a race with him!"

"Huh!" Mabel sneered, "fat chance you'd have of beating *him*! Why, he's the fastest runner on the ball team!"

"Well, I don't care if he is," was the answer. "I'd like to try it just the same."

"Pooh! You think because you beat Bert once in a while you can beat *anybody*."

"I do not!" denied Millie, "But I'll bet a quarter I can beat you, Mabel Pecoy."

"Well, I haven't got any quarter to bet, and betting isn't nice anyway, but if I *did* bet, I wouldn't be afraid to race you, so there!"

"All right, smarty, let's try it. I bet I can beat you round that road down there," and she pointed to the race track which circled the ball field.

"Why Millie!" Josie exclaimed. "That's where they have the horse races when they have the fall fair! It's half a mile round it – you couldn't run half a mile!"

"Don't' s'pose I could," Millie acknowledged, "but it's a dandy place to run on, and we could race till one had to stop, couldn't we?"

"I know, but Millie! Right in front of all these people? The idea! Don't do it – please don't," and Josie looked terribly distressed.

But Millie's dander was up, and so was Mabel's, who snapped, "I don't care if all the people in town are here! Prob'ly Boston folks might, but I don't."

"Neither do I," Millie replied, angered at Mabel's slur, and she ran down to the track, followed by her opponent.

The group in the stand was divided, some urging the two girls on, some expostulating, but all much excited at the prospect of a race. "I'll count three," said Millie. "Now don't you start till you hear three," and Mabel, forcefully, although inelegantly answered, "Oh shut up! I know how to run a race as well as you do."

"All right, Miss Smarty. Ready One-two-three-GO!" Millie had counted rapidly, probably thinking she would catch her rival unawares, but she didn't, for in a split second after "go," Mabel was half a rod down the track.

Perhaps Mabel knew how to run a race, but she was making the mistake in this one, of running at her very best pace right from the start, her arms flying in all directions. Millie happened to remember that she should take it easy at first, saving her best efforts for the wind up, having been instructed by both Bert and Frank, and also that she should keep her arms close to her ribs. So, regardless of Mabel's lead, she jogged along steadily, trying to breathe easily, and remember about her arms.

The whole crowd of on-lookers was on its feet the moment the girls were off, and the ball players were yelling like demons, mostly for Mabel, which was natural enough, she being a schoolmate.

But Bill was remembering the cheer the Boston girl had given him, and suddenly he left the group of boys, and with a wild howl of "GO IT, BOSTON!" he cut across the field, running abreast of her, but keeping inside the track.

Millie was too intent on her running to see who it was, or hear what he was saying, and ran on doggedly, slowly but surely gaining on Mabel. They were about a third of the way round the track, and Mabel was pretty nearly winded, when suddenly she gave out entirely and stopped, panting for breath. With one final burst of speed, Millie passed her, ran a little further, and stopped.

Rejoining Mabel, who was laughing and apparently holding no grudge, they started back across the field toward their companions. It was then that Millie discovered that her "pacer" had been "that boy," and that he too had turned and was on his way back to the group of ball players.

When he reached them Dubois shook his hand sadly, and said, "Why, ole Bill! I'm surprised at you! Running after a Boston girl! What's the matter with our own girls?" And then as Bill only laughed, he went on, "Did you get near enough to get a good look?"

Bill laughed again, and replied, "Sure I did. I got *two* good looks. 'Course she ain't as pretty as Nattie Bell is, but you better not let Nattie know you're so interested in another girl's looks!" And the laugh was turned on Dubois, for they all knew that he was Nattie's school "beau."

Admissions were collected during the intermission, and there was no further excitement other than the game itself. It was a close game all the way; a tie in the eighth, but Goffstown was one up at the end of the ninth.

The New Boston players and visitors drifted back to the waiting buses, not as ebullient and boisterous as on their arrival, but vowing a return the next month and wreaking vengeance.

Most of the Goffstowners had left, too, leaving a few enthusiasts to rehash the various plays and rejoice over the final outcome.

Bert and Frank announced that they were leaving, and going back the way they had come, and the four Paige Hill girls debated as to whether they should try it too, or go round by the Village.

Millie settled the matter by saying, "Oh come on, let's go round by the Village and I'll treat to sodas. I'm thirsty. Hey, you too, Mabel," she added hastily, as Mabel started ahead. So the boys went off toward the river, and the girls left for the promised treat.

Most of the ball players had left for the river and a swim after their strenuous afternoon, but Bill had managed to elude them and was not far behind the four girls. He hurried a little to catch up with them and spoke to Josie, grinned at Jennie, and opened conversation with Mabel and Millie by complimenting them on their race. He wasn't much of a "looker," Millie thought to herself, but she rather liked his freckled face, his shining merry brown eyes, and his infectious grin.

The conversation became general, although in some manner three of the girls were in the vanguard, while Bill, tossing his baseball up and catching it, walked behind – with Millie. He was thinking of *her* looks, too, and decided that while she wasn't at all pretty, but what of it? He liked her looks, and her easy, friendly way – so that was that.

As they turned at Carr's Corner, he managed to slow up a little, dropping a bit further behind the others and naturally she followed suit. And presently, stammering a little, Bill said, "Say, how about stopping at Ote Sumner's for a glass of soda?"

Now soda was nothing new to Millie, and neither were boys, but even so, this was the first time she had ever been asked to have a soda *with* a boy, so naturally she got quite a thrill out of the invitation! However she did not show it, and with great aplomb, replied, "All right. I'd like one, thank you. I'm awfully thirsty."

And then she thought of her invitation to treat the girls! For a moment she did not know just what to do in a case like this, but being resourceful, she went on calmly, "Wait here a minute, Bill. I want to speak to Josie." She ran ahead to the three girls and said in a low voice." Here, Josie, here's a quarter. You go get the sodas for you and the girls."

"Why, where are you going?" Josie asked, surprised, but accepting the quarter.

"Oh, I'll be there," was the nonchalant reply. "Bill what's-his-name asked me to have one with him. Wait for me after, though." She added and dropped back to Bill, leaving the girls speechless with surprise at such an event.

Bill and Millie drank their sodas at one of the two small tables. The others, standing at the fountain, eyed them; Josie amazed at Millie's self possession, Mabel with disinterest, giving her attention mostly to the soda, and Jennie with an unblinking stare, until Bill winked at her wickedly, causing her to choke over her drink, and blush violently.

After a while, the last drop was drained, and they left the store, as before, the three in front, and the two, now quite friendly and well acquainted, following.

As they turned down Elm Street, Bill said, "Does Mis' Paige let you girls have company?"

"'Course she does," Millie replied, surprised. "She *likes* company, and somebody's there 'bout every day. We have awful good times. Why? You comin' up?"

"Well," he answered, considering this almost an invitation, "Sometimes my father lets me take ole Charles, if he hasn't worked too hard – Charles I mean – so I thought maybe I could drive up some evenin', - if you wouldn't mind."

"No, I wouldn't mind. I'd like to have you – we all would." And then she surprised him by adding, "When you comin'?"

Bill laughed and said, "Well – er—how about tonight, after supper?" He wondered if she would think he was rushing things a little, but evidently she didn't mind that either, for she said, "P'haps he won't let you have ole Charles, tonight."

"Oh well," Bill returned, "if he won't – I'll be up anyway. I'll walk."

They both laughed, but Millie said, warningly, "Well, all right, only you better come early, 'cause Josie and I have to go to bed at nine o'clock."

"All right," was the reply. "I won't stay after nine. Here's where I live" he added, and stopped before a large white house, almost at the end of the Village.

The three girls were waiting at the front walk, talking to a girl about Bert's age, and who looked like Bill. "This is my sister Carrie," he said, and then hesitated, for he did not know Millie's last name. But Josie came to the rescue by saying, "and this is Millie Rumney, Carrie. She stays at our house summers," thus completing the introduction.

They chatted a moment longer, but Millie seemed anxious to go on, so they said good-bye and started off on the mile walk home.

Millie set rather a speedy pace, and finally Josie said, "Hey, what's your hurry?" and Jennie added, puffing for breath, "My goodness, you running another race?"

"No," was the reply, her pace not slacking up in the least. And then she capped the climax to an exciting afternoon, by remarking off-handedly, "No, I'm not running any race, but we better move along just the same. It's after five now and supper to eat, Bill's comin' up tonight!"

EDITORS NOTE: Mildred Rumney married William B. Morgrage on the 30th of April, 1907. William died on the 22nd of August, 1921 and Millie lived in the Morgrage home with her sister-in-law, Carrie for many years thereafter. The Morgrage home must have been bought by Carrie's husband Fred Stark, for I was always under the assumption that it was the Stark home, not a Morgrage home. Carrie and Fred were my grandparents and Aunt Millie lived in their home until she was moved into a nursing home in Manchester. I remember her as a little old lady, sitting in a rocking chair working on a quilt, or mending or sewing on something, always with a sad little smile on her face. Maybe she was remembering all the good times she had had in Goffstown as a child and thinking up just one more scheme to play on someone.

Nancy Stephenson